Guide to
Successful Bass Fishing

GUIDE TO SUCCESSFUL BASS FISHING

Today's Newest and Most Effective Techniques:

Pinpointing Lunkers
Conquering New Waters
An Accurate Day-by-day Guide
Predicting Prime Feeding Times
Determining the Best Days for a Trophy
The Latest *Scientific* Facts of Bass Behavior
...and Much More!

by

Rick Taylor

MOUNTAIN PRESS PUBLISHING COMPANY
MISSOULA, MONTANA
1979

© Copyright 1979
Mountain Press Publishing Co.

Library of Congress Cataloging in Publication Data

Taylor, Rick.
  Guide to successful bass fishing.

  Bibliography: p.
  Includes index.
  1. Largemouth bass fishing.   I. Title.
SH681.T37   798.1'7'58   79-9752
ISBN 0-87842-113-0
ISBN 0-87842-115-7 pbk.
Second printing January 1984

Dedication

With love and gratitude this book is dedicated to:

Dr. Wendel Taylor
for his example

Helen Taylor
for her spiritual support

Kris Taylor
for her loving patience

Acknowledgments

I offer my special thanks to:
Bob Cobb, editor of *Bassmaster* Magazine,
Jack Samson, editor of *Field & Stream* Magazine
and Ted Kesting, editor of *Sports Afield* Magazine
for permission to use several illustrations and
portions of text previously appearing under my byline
in one or more of their respective publications;

Lowrance Electronics, Fishhawk Electronics,
Plastics Research and Development
and Fin & Feather Sports Center in Iowa City
for donations of quality equipment to my research;

Lloyd Bender for his invaluable assistance
in the preparation of this book's photographs;

and to hundreds of fellow bass fishermen I have met
over the years who, through their willingness
to share information, have made my job easier
and even more enjoyable.

CONTENTS

Preface

One of the first prerequisites to successful bass fishing is to recognize which aspects are the most important, and then channel your energies in those directions. Many potentially good anglers place too much emphasis on things like lure selection and manipulation before they have even begun to master the more vital elements. You probably have only so much time to devote to this pleasurable sport, so why not spend it where it will do the most good?

That's why this book deals largely with *finding the bass*. There simply is nothing more important. No one short of Deity can catch fish from where none exists, and it's a cruel fact that at least 90 percent of any body of water is bassless.

A close second, however, is *being there when they are hitting*. Even experts bow more often than you think to tight-lipped bass, no matter how well placed or presented the lures. While, on the reverse, few things can erase a neophyte's inexperience like bass on a careless feeding spree. Without a doubt, certain days and certain hours of any day are better than others for catching bass. And for those of you on a time budget, we'll see how to predict many of them well in advance.

The "how" — namely lure choice and presentation — is discussed at times. Occasionally, bass have their sights on just one or two species of prey, and if you don't offer the right lure in the right way, you may find nothing dangling from the hooks. But since every lake, bass and situation is different, the best way is still trial and error. All I or anyone can offer is a few good starting places.

Concentrating on the more important fields is one way this book separates itself from others. Another, perhaps, is the way I researched it. Rather than write from just the experience of experts, or from scientific facts, or underwater observations, etc., I tried to tap them all thoroughly. I felt this was the best way to put together an *accurate* system for understanding and catching bass — one that would help anyone, regardless of where he lives, the types of waters he fishes or how skilled he presently is. Zeroing in on just one or two areas would surely limit this book's scope and make the information too regional.

To date, this fulltime endeavor has spanned seven enjoyable years. A good share of that has been spent consulting the most reliable (and ignored) source we fishermen have: *science*. Collectively, fisheries biologists and researchers have discovered more about fish and fishing than any thousand anglers could ever hope to in as many lifetimes. Most scientists have devoted their lives to their work. They are well equipped, they work under carefully controlled conditions and freely exchange data with colleagues — all with one common goal: to uncover the truth. The larger university libraries are stacked high with their findings. What I found there concerning bass behavior is so sound, it has become the very foundation of this book.

I also found a quality resource in the heads of expert bass fishermen. Not just one or two, mind you, but the combined experience of many. By fishing with, interviewing and closely studying masters from the north, the south, the big impoundments, the ponds, fellow angling writers and tournament professionals, I have seen many definite patterns for angling success emerge.

Then, of course, there has been my own fishing experience. As you may suspect of someone in this line of work, I'm on the water a lot and I keep very detailed fishing logs. But that's only part of it. Because bass tournaments are like having my own army of researchers on the lake at once, I fish many each year. I also conduct numerous experiments in bass behavior and constantly monitor the major variables of water and weather. Occasionally I work with divers and I go shocking with fisheries biologists at every opportunity. In other words, I'm not a reporter, blindly passing along tips gleaned from others. Practically every piece of information in this book has had to prove its bass-catching worth through me — being checked against the facts of science, the concensus of many top anglers and my own personal testing.

The final, unique feature of this book is its presentation. Part One is devoted to the facts and supported theories of the more important variables — temperature, oxygen, food, light and structure — and a few of the lesser ones. You will see what effect each has on the largemouth, how he responds to it and how it can vary throughout a body of water from season to season, day to day and hour to hour. Call it a "reference section of facts," designed especially for those who prefer thinking for themselves...like a bass.

The tips and methods begin with Part Two. But even here I try to present the "why" along with the "how." You'll see techniques like how to determine the best times to go fishing, finding the bass' best depths and much more...all with a scientific basis.

Then in Part Three the facts, theories, tips and techniques all come together to form a fundamental guide. Based on water temperature rather than calendar dates, it should help you locate and catch largemouths year-round on just about any body of water in the country.

With no surprise to you nor embarassment to me, the following pages do not contain all the answers. We still have so much to learn about this fantastic fish. And what is considered fact today may be obsolete tomorrow, due to the largemouth's remarkable ability to alter his behavior in the face of an ever-changing environment. Consequently, this book concentrates mostly on those stable, consistent factors which apply to bass *in general* today and, therefore, should hold for many years to come. Since true bass fishing expertise can come only from personal experience, I believe this offers you the best possible foundation to build upon.

PART ONE
THE FACTS

This section is dedicated to bass fishermen who want to know "why," not just "how." Bless your hearts.

The Variables

Bass are ruled largely by the iron hand of their environment. While they follow certain internal laws such as hunger, survival instincts and reproduction, where they are at any given moment and their willingness to take a lure at that time are regulated mostly by environmental factors, more commonly called "variables." By studying the most important of these, we can unlock many secrets of the bass.

The five major variables governing largemouths are:
- Water Temperature
- Oxygen
- Food
- Light
- Structure (cover)

Where the best combination of these is found under the surface, so will be the majority of adult bass. And in line with the same principle, *when these variables are most favorable to the bass for feeding, you should have the best chance of catching them.*

So before making your first cast, gather as much information as possible about each variable, then put it all together to organize a game plan. The time this will save you can be tremendous. Every day and every lake is different, and studying the environmental factors is the surest, fastest way to figure out the bass.

Chapter 1
Water Temperature

The only time water temperature concerns some anglers is when they fall overboard. But to the conscientious bass stalker, few things are more important. In a sense, it's the bass' bible, telling him where to go, what to do and when to do it. It often plays a role in his depth selection, how frequently he will feed, when his spawning cycle will begin and end, and even what lures will work best and the proper speed to present them. Learning the facts of and keeping in touch with water temperature will definitely make you a better bass fisherman.

METABOLISM

Warm-blooded creatures, such as you and I, have a fairly constant body temperature, whether we are frying on a 95-degree beach or turning blue at 20 below zero, ice fishing. Cold-blooded animals, like bass, will have a body temperature approximately the same as their immediate surroundings. Because of this, water temperature is the major force regulating a

3

bass' activity — or in biological terminology, his metabolism. Up to a point, the warmer the water, the faster his metabolic rate, and therefore the more active he will be. The colder the water, the slower his life proceeds, even to the point of dormancy. Consequently, the amount and type of food a bass consumes in a given time, the time it takes to digest it and sometimes even the time of day he feeds all depend largely on his metabolic rate, which in turn hinges mostly on the temperature of the water he is in.

THE IDEAL TEMPERATURE

From what we just discussed, it's easy to see why some people believe bass do not have a preferred temperature. It's logical to assume that if a bass is "comfortable" in any temperature, there is no force driving him to find a specific one. Science, however, has proven conclusively that practically all freshwater species do have an ideal temperature.

To find out what it is for largemouth bass from the northern part of the United States, scientists placed a number of identically-sized bass in aquariums with different water temperatures, ranging from 50 to 80 degrees. Over the course of a year they were all offered the same number of minnows each day. By the end of the test the bass in the *68 degree tank* had eaten the most, used that nutrition best and, therefore, weighed more than any of their comrades. It was concluded that 68 degrees was the ideal temperature for these northern largemouths.

A similar study on bass from mid-America revealed their best temperature was 72 degrees. And one that was done in Texas (the deep South) showed the ideal to be 75-76 degrees. As you can see, the exact temperature at which a bass' body operates at peak performance depends on the average temperature of his water — or the "thermal history" as limnologists call it. A typical lake in Minnesota, for example, would have a relatively cool yearly average. Bass there will perform best in 67-69 degrees, because water warmer than this seldom exists at times other than the heat of summer. Throw those same bass into a much warmer lake, say in Alabama, and their ideal temperature will eventually move up to 73-75 degrees.

SEEKING THE IDEAL TEMPERATURE

So, if bass do have one specific ideal temperature, will they actively seek it out? The answer is yes. Many studies have verified this, but the following is one of the more convincing.

Ten groups of equally-sized largemouths were placed in ten aquariums, each with a different water temperature — 40 degrees, 45, 50 and so on up to 85 degrees. Once all were acclimated to their various temperatures, one by one they were transferred to a much larger aquarium offering a wide range of temperatures from 50 to 80 degrees. Whatever temperature the bass swam to and remained in was recorded, then he was removed and the next contestant brought in. Figure 1 shows the results on these mid-America largemouths.

BASS ACCLIMATED TO THIS TEMPERATURE		SWAM TO THIS WHEN GIVEN A CHOICE
40°		54° (+14)
45°		59° (+14)
50°		64° (+14)
55°		67° (+12)
60°		68° (+ 8)
65°		71° (+ 6)
70°		72° (+ 2)
75°		73° (− 2)
80°		74° (− 6)
85°		75° (−10)

Figure 1. Temperature Selection of Mid-America Largemouths. Given a choice, these bass headed for an ideal temperature of 72-73 degrees, generally avoiding a sudden change that would be too much of a shock.

For example, the bass which had been held in the 40-degree tank swam to and remained in the 54-degree water, once given a choice. Those from the 45-degree tank preferred the 59-degree layer. Those from 50 degrees went to 64 degrees, and so on. The fact that the bass from the colder-water tanks always chose a much warmer temperature hints that they were "on their way" to a specific ideal. They didn't go for it immediately, because the sudden jump would have been too much of a shock. Fish need roughly 24 hours to condition themselves to a new, higher water temperature.

More proof comes when we look at the temperature selection of the bass from the warmer 75, 80 and 85-degree holding tanks. In all three instances the temperature chosen was *cooler* than what they had been acclimated to — 73, 74 and 75 degrees were their respective choices. Since all other variables (oxygen, light, cover, etc.) were kept constant throughout this experiment, the only conclusion to draw is that these mid-America bass wanted to be in their ideal temperature of 72-73 degrees. And if given sufficient time (a day or two) for complete adjustment, all would have settled there eventually.

Of course, as we learned earlier, if these largemouths had come from the northern part of the country, they would probably have selected a cooler ideal, and if from the South, a warmer one. The size of the fish also makes a difference. As a rule, the smaller the bass, the less important an ideal temperature is — or perhaps it would be more accurate to say the wider his range of preference. This is because in relation to body size the gills of a one-pounder, for example, are much larger than the gills of a five-pound bass. More oxygen can pass through the smaller fish's gills and thereby keep him more comfortable in warmer waters where more oxygen is required. This is why in mid-summer, when the bass are supposed to be deep, you often see small ones skittering around in the shallows, even when the temperature there is 85 degrees or more. Their bodies require more oxygen in the warmer water, but their gills can provide it.

MAXIMUM TEMPERATURES

From these studies it's obvious that if bass had their way, they'd spend all their lives in the ideal temperature. Unfortunately, this isn't possible, because in the colder months of fall, winter and early spring the water is usually well below that ideal. Even during much of summer, when it does exist, they have to leave it to feed. Just about everything tasty to a bass prefers a warmer temperature than he, so if he doesn't move into the warmer shallows where they are, his career as a bass will be short-lived.

When the shallows themselves are close to the bass' ideal temperature, he'll spend great lengths of time there ambushing prey. But as summer progresses and the shallows heat up well past the ideal, bass will retreat to cooler depths and make short trips back to the shallows for feeding. It's important to us, therefore, that we know how warm he can stand the water and how long he'll stay in it for feeding. This is difficult to pinpoint exactly, because the current oxygen supply plays a critical role. But the following experiment should give us a fair idea.

Bass in aquariums were observed as the temperature of their water was slowly increased past their ideal. For the first eight

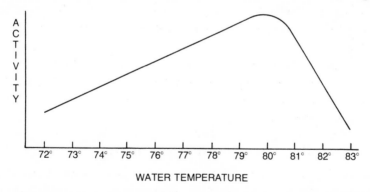

WATER TEMPERATURE

Figure 2. Maximum High Temperature Comfortable to a Three-Pound Largemouth Bass Acclimated to 72 Degrees. The bass steadily became more active as the aquarium water was warmed from 72 to 80 degrees. Beyond that he showed a sudden decrease in movement, and respiration increased.

degrees their activity increased linearly. From then on it began to drop off. (See Figure 2.) If, for example, the bass' ideal was 72 degrees, apparently 80 degrees (72+8) is about the maximum he'll remain in for more than a few minutes. Any warmer and he would become sluggish.

This poses an interesting question: If water over 80 degrees makes bass sluggish, how can they ever feed successfully during those hot days of summer? One answer is that it takes *20 minutes* for a fish's body, regardless of size, to take on the temperature of warmer or colder water. This gives crafty bass a chance to pick off a couple morsels before having to retreat back to the cooler, more compatible depths. For this reason fishing action often comes in short bursts on a summer day.

Another answer is that a bass' ideal temperature usually rises during summer to compensate for warmer water. Again, let's say his true ideal is 72 degrees. As summer progresses and the water heats up, that 72-degree layer he is so fond of is pushed deeper and deeper. Our bass will probably "follow" it down at first, but by mid-summer it may have travelled deeper than he cares to go, being too far from his shallow-water feeding grounds. That's when he will probably level off and start putting up with warmer water. His body will soon adjust and, in a sense, that higher temperature will become his new temporary ideal, as long as it is no more than about three degrees higher than the original. In this case that means 75 degrees (72 +3). And with a three-degree higher ideal, theoretically his maximum temperature will also be three degrees higher. Our bass could now remain in 83-degree water (rather than 80) for extended periods.

Unfortunately, sometimes the shallow-water feeding grounds just get too hot. If they don't cool back down to a compatible level at night, the bass may have little choice but to forego feeding in the shallows altogether until conditions improve. A partner in crime is usually poor oxygen, and together they generate one of the bass fisherman's worst nemeses — summer "dog days."

WEATHER'S EFFECT ON WATER TEMPERATURE

Thermal changes occur in a body of water not just seasonally, but daily and hourly as well, thanks amost entirely to the weather. These fluctuations often trigger new behavior patterns in bass, and if you have a working knowledge of weather and water temperature, you can sometimes predict the bass' move before he makes it.

We'll begin with a fundamental look at seasonal changes in a lake's temperature, then inspect those occurring more frequently. For the advanced angler, some of this will be a refresher course. But for beginners, it's helpful, basic reading.

THE SEASONS

The thermal condition of a lake or pond during winter is relatively uncomplicated since there's little change from top to bottom. One of our southern lakes, for example, may have a

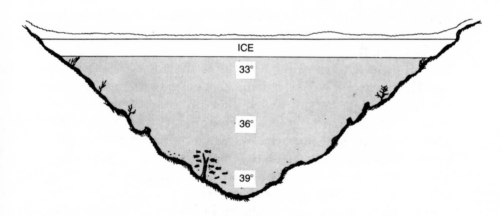

Figure 3. Thermal Stratification of Lake Under Ice. This is the only condition in which a fish finds warmer water the deeper he goes.

uniform temperature of 45 degrees. Occasional attacks of abnormal weather can cause minor variations, but for the most part the uniformity will continue on through winter.

In our typical northern lakes, where ice forms every year, things are different. Just before ice-out, such a lake would be thermally stratified. (See Figure 3.)

Note that the deeper you go, the warmer it gets. This is a strange phenomenon of nature, because normally, water, like air, rises as it warms and sinks as it cools. In summer you'll find a lake's warmest temperature at the surface and the coldest at the bottom. Under ice, however, it's the complete opposite. Water reaches its maximum density at 39.1 degrees, which means it has become as heavy as it will get. As it gets even colder — approaching the freezing point of 32 degrees — it becomes *lighter*. This is why ice floats. If it didn't, many of our lakes would freeze solid in winter and kill everything in it.

As spring approaches, warming air temperatures and increasing winds remove the ice. Shortly, the surface will warm to the same temperature as the bottom, creating a thermal uniformity much the same as a southern lake experienced all winter long. At this point, even a moderate wind will mix the entire lake from top to bottom, resulting in what is known as "spring turnover."

"Turnover" will continue as long as the stiff spring winds, usually four to six weeks. During this period the upper layers are warmed by the sun and higher air temperatures, then mixed throughout the lake by wind-produced currents. This keeps the entire lake uniform. But when the winds subside, the mixing does also. Now, when the upper layers warm, there are no currents strong enough to mix them in with the colder bottom regions. This causes a layering or "stratification" of water temperatures, such as shown in Figure 4. Once stratification pretty well sets in, the bottom layers become sealed off. Only a very strong wind will be capable of mixing them with the upper regions, because their difference in temperature — and thus density — is too great.

10

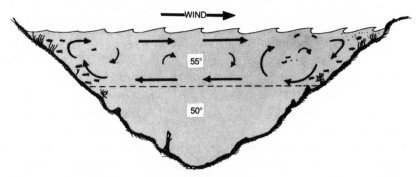

Figure 4. End of Spring Turnover. During a calm sunny day the upper region became warmer (and therefore less dense) than the lower region; the difference in densities now keeps the two from mixing when winds spring up . . .unless the wind is very strong.

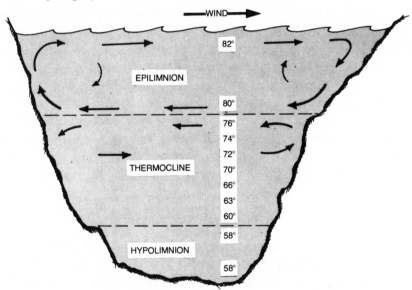

Figure 5. Summer Stratification of a Deep Lake. The upper layers are mixed by winds, causing their temperature to stay relatively uniform. The middle layers have mild currents, but their strong thermal stratification keeps them separate from the upper layers. The lower layers are also uniform, because this water is virtually dead and sealed off from the rest of the lake. Poor oxygen may develop here in late summer, unless the water is infertile.

Figure 5 shows what a deep lake may look like during summer. The upper region, called the *epilimnion,* has a warm, fairly uniform temperature and continues to mix with itself, just as the entire lake did during spring turnover. The middle layer is called the *thermocline,* and is characterized by a cooler, non-uniform temperature. In fact, the temperature usually drops in the neighborhood of at least one degree for every foot you descend. You will probaby find the resting area of most adult gamefish here, because it contains their ideal temperatures. The bottom region, the *hypolimnion,* is important to us only in that it is an unlikely place for our quarry to be. It is cold and quite often too poor in oxygen to support life for any length of time. As a rule, only very deep lakes will have a hypolimnion.

Summer turns into fall, the air cools and the winds crank up once again. The warm upper regions — the epilimnion — begin cooling and becoming more dense. Soon they are as cool as the water in the thermocline, and the two will mix readily. After more cooling and bad weather there may be little difference between the surface and the bottom. Along comes a stout breeze and the entire lake mixes together once again. You guessed it, this phase is called "fall turnover." In our northern lakes it will continue until ice forms and seals the water from the wind. The result is where we started — winter stratification.

DAILY CHANGES

As we've seen, sunlight and air temperature are the two main contributors of heat or cold to a body of water. Yet the immediate effect of either depends largely on the wind. For instance, on a calm, clear day, heat from the sun can penetrate full force into the upper layers of a lake, causing the surface to warm as much as ten degrees. However, from say five feet on down, depending on the water's clarity, the temperature will rise much less because the shallows absorbed all the incoming heat. (See "A" in Figure 6.)

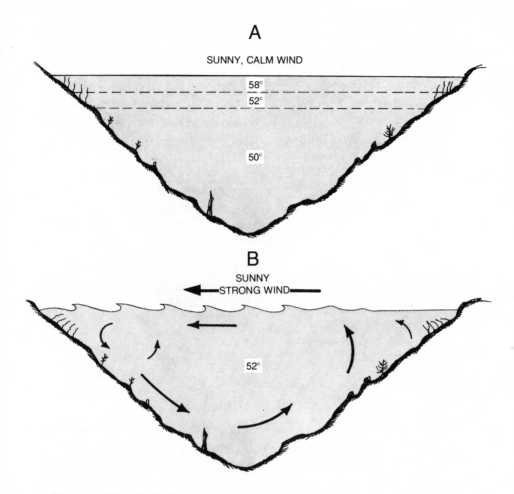

A

SUNNY, CALM WIND

58°

52°

50°

B

SUNNY
STRONG WIND

52°

Figure 6. The Role Wind Plays in Water Temperature Variation and Distribution. Two identical situations, except in one the wind is calm, in the other it is strong.

A wind in this situation would change things considerably. Waves breaking along an otherwise glassy surface would scatter the sun's heat back into the air, thereby allowing much less to penetrate into the water. It would also produce currents, which could carry what heat the shallows did gain down to mix with the colder depths. (See "B" in Figure 6.)

13

Wind controls the air temperature's effect on water in much the same way. As those waves roll across the surface, they pull in heat or cold from the air and mix it into the water. The stronger the wind, the faster the heat exchange and the more thorough the mixing — and, of course, the greater the difference between air and water temperatures, the more radical the change. With no wind, the temperature of the air will have little effect on the temperature of the water, regardless of their differences.

Fishhawk 530
Electronic
Thermometer

ELECTRONIC THERMOMETERS

To find the depth at which a bass' ideal temperature occurs, and to keep tabs on the overall thermal condition of the water, there is only one type of thermometer that does the job. This is the electronic thermometer made especially for fishermen. It costs anywhere from $20 to $60 and most are worth the investment. The two things to look for in one are accuracy and spontaneity. The reason accuracy is important need not be explained. Spontaneity is often overlooked. If your thermometer does not give an instant readout, you may waste valuable time recording water temperatures. With one that registers its findings instantly, you can record a lake's temperature from top to bottom in about a minute, even if there's a change at every foot, such as during summer stratification.

14

HOURLY VARIATIONS
July 3; Sunny, Calm, 84°

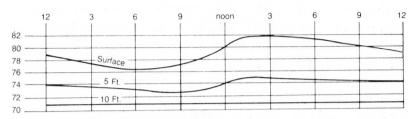

WEEKLY VARIATIONS

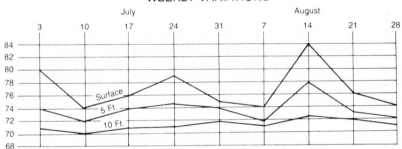

MONTHLY VARIATIONS

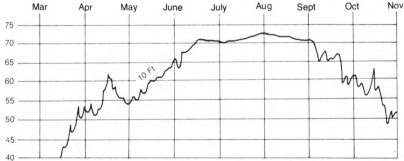

Figure 7. How Water Temperature Varies at Different Depths Over Different Periods of Time. Notice that the deeper the water, the more stable it usually is.

15

SUMMARY

Water temperature is important to bass fishermen because it regulates the bass' bodily functions (metabolism). Every bass has a specific temperature in which his body operates best. Roughly this is 68 degrees in the northern United States, 72 degrees for mid-America bass and 75 degrees in the South.

With other variables being favorable and therefore not factors, bass actively seek out and remain in this ideal temperature. However, they sometimes must leave it to feed, remain closer to the food or to avoid poor oxygen. As a rule, the smaller the bass, the less he is affected by temperatures warmer than his ideal.

Water approximately eight degrees warmer than his ideal is the maximum a bass will remain in for more than a few minutes. When his shallow-water feeding grounds become too warm during summer, he will probably come to them for only a few minutes at a time, spending the rest of his day in the cooler depths. These visits are made possible by the fact that it takes his body 20 minutes to assume the temperature of warmer or colder water. In warm bodies of water a bass' ideal temperature may rise a few degrees during summer to compensate for the hotter periods. If conditions become too severe, bass usually turn off until they improve. In colder months, bodies of water are relatively uniform in temperature. From late spring to early fall they usually stratify, creating distinct thermal layers. The warmer upper layers react to weather conditions (wind, sun, air temperature) while deeper layers are sealed off, and therefore change little thermally day to day.

Sun and air temperatures are the two main contributors of heat and cold to water. The effect of either depends on the strength of the wind. When the wind is calm, heat from the sun can penetrate fully into the upper layers, causing them to warm as much as 10 degrees. When the wind is blowing, wave action scatters this heat back into the air, so little is gained from the sun. But these waves pull in heat or cold from the air and mix it into the water.

Chapter 2
Oxygen

Unlike electronic thermometers, the oxygen monitor's debut into bass fishing was met with just so-so enthusiasm. Many anglers were just getting the hang of water temperature and didn't need another innovation so soon. Others remained more open minded until they discovered the price of these new gadgets. Then their minds and wallets slammed shut. Of those that did make the investment, some found the monitor delightfully helpful, while others ranked it with rubber hooks.

Why the difference in opinion? Is an oxygen monitor worth the money? And if so, how does it work? Hopefully, this chapter will answer these questions and more.

HOW MUCH OXYGEN BASS REQUIRE

It is generally accepted that bass must have an oxygen content of between 6 ppm (parts per million) and 14 ppm. Some feel this range is 5 to 13 ppm, but it's only because no two lakes — and therefore groups of bass — are exactly the same. The lake's location, average water temperature, clarity and a half dozen other factors all help design a bass' preferences. For simplicity's sake, we'll just say that any water containing less than 5 ppm or more than 14 ppm can cause them to become less active, even die if it drops below 2 or 1 ppm. More than 14 ppm can cause oxygen poisoning in the fish's blood.

This range gives us a nice place to start, but in most situations it's too broad to be much help, since 5-14 ppm can easily cover every cubic foot of water in an entire lake. Fortunately, like temperature, the oxygen preference of bass can be narrowed down considerably, and in doing so, help us zero in on their most likely feeding and resting depths. Let's begin by looking at the three main factors deciding how much oxygen a bass needs at any given moment:

—his size

—his present state of activity (feeding versus resting)

—most important, the temperature of the water he is in.

Figure 8 illustrates this.

Right away you'll notice that the warmer the water, the more oxygen a bass needs. As we saw in the previous chapter, a fish's metabolism is controlled mostly by water temperature: the warmer the water, the faster his gears grind, and the more fuel (oxygen) he requres.

Next, it's obvious that a feeding bass needs more oxygen than a resting one. While taking it easy in a non-feeding mood, a bass' rhythm is relatively slow. But come dinnertime his metabolism automatically fires up, even if he just lies there and ambushes. So, of course, more oxygen is needed, especially if his feed is successful, as digestion puts even more demand on oxygen intake.

Finally, notice the difference size makes. As a rule, the bigger the bass, the more oxygen he needs for feeding, yet the less he requires for resting. This may sound contradictory, but it's easily explained. Compared to a 10-inch bass, a lunker's gills are smaller in relation to body size. So once that hulk fires up for feeding, it takes a lot of gas to move it around (like a

18

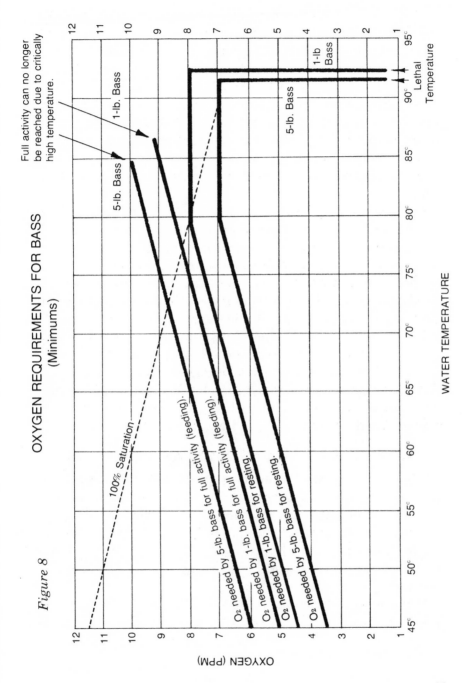

Figure 8

OXYGEN REQUIREMENTS FOR BASS
(Minimums)

OXYGEN (PPM)

WATER TEMPERATURE

Full activity can no longer be reached due to critically high temperature.

5-lb. Bass

1-lb. Bass

1-lb Bass

5-lb. Bass

Lethal Temperature

100% Saturation

O₂ needed by 5-lb. bass for full activity (feeding).
O₂ needed by 1-lb. bass for full activity (feeding).
O₂ needed by 1-lb. bass for resting.
O₂ needed by 5-lb. bass for resting.

Cadillac and a VW travelling at the same speed). And with his relatively small gills, a higher concentration of oxygen must pass through them to fulfill a lunker's requirements.

The reason a big bass needs less for resting is because he can control his metabolism better than a small bass. The latter are almost always moving, to the point where there is little difference between their resting and feeding states. Big bass, on the other hand, are very good at shutting themselves down to a greatly reduced metabolic rate when necessary. This explains why the smallest fish often die first in a critical oxygen situation.

Don't worry about memorizing these facts and figures. Figure 9 shows the same thing as Figure 8, only in a condensed, quick-reference form. It doesn't cover water colder than 70 degrees, because water below this temperature invariably has all the oxygen any fish could ever need. A good fact to always remember is that the colder the water, the more oxygen it can (and probably does) hold. At 60 degrees, for example, you'll notice in Figure 8 that 100 percent saturation (the most oxygen water can hold before giving some back to the air) is almost 10ppm. That's way above a bass' requirement for any activity. Knowing each degree's "saturation level" is not vitally important, but this line on the chart helps illustrate why oxygen is seldom worth considering any time other than summer.

HOW OXYGEN VARIES IN LAKES AND PONDS

When I first began digging through the mounds of scientific data on oxygen, I ran across an interesting observation made by a limnologist. He said, in effect, "A study of a lake's oxygen can tell more about that lake and its fish than any other single factor." Not only was I later to find other scientists agreeing with this, but myself as well, through my own experiments and research.

While water temperature is what scientists call a "controlling factor" telling bass where to go, what to do and when to do

Figure 9   APPROXIMATE OXYGEN REQUIREMENTS
OF LARGEMOUTH BASS
(Minimums)

	5-LB. BASS		1-LB. BASS	
TEMP.	RESTING	FEEDING	RESTING	FEEDING
70	6 PPM	8½ PPM	7 PPM	7½ PPM
75	6½ PPM	9 PPM	7½ PPM	8 PPM
80	7 PPM	9½ PPM	8 PPM	8½ PPM
85	7 PPM	10 PPM	8 PPM	9 PPM
90	7 PPM		8 PPM	

it, oxygen is a "limiting factor" telling bass whether or not they can do it. Sometimes the oxygen supply of a body of water is so good it is of no concern whatsoever to the bass or us. Other times it may be so poor that it becomes the only concern to both. In most bodies of water both extremes exist simultaneously during the warmer months. One cove may have 10 ppm — enough for all-out feeding — while another has only 6 ppm — barely enough for resting. One week the bass may be living comfortably at 20 feet in 8 ppm of oxygen, then next they are forced into the shallows just to keep from suffocating.

Oxygen Sources. Water obtains its oxygen from two sources: certain microscopic plants called "plankton" and from the air. The amount it can hold depends largely on its temperature and clarity; and how this oxygen is distributed is controlled by the wind. Let's look at these one at a time.

When the right intensity of sunlight strikes those little green specks suspended in the water, they begin eating up carbon dioxide and spitting out oxygen. When sunlight is not present, the reverse happens. This keeps the oxygen supply fluctuating, being lowest at dawn after many hours of darkness, and highest around mid-to-late afternoon as the sun concludes its four or so hours of brightest intensity and deepest

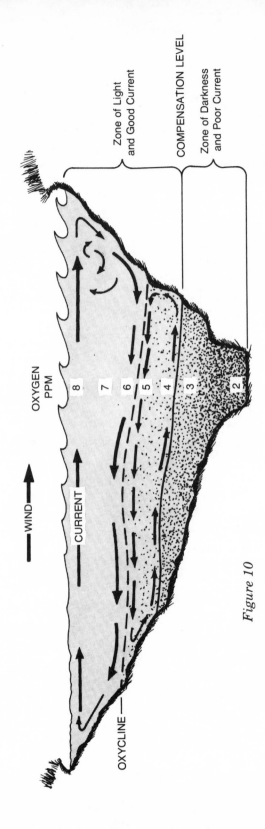

Figure 10

penetration. Of course, the oxygen production by plankton will be somewhat tempered when clouds, dirty water or wave action inhibit the amount of sunlight entering the water.

Water can also pull fresh oxygen from the air. In fact, during colder months when the water temperature is below 60 degrees and relatively little plankton exists, this is its major supplier. Water and air are continuously trying to stay balanced with each other in oxygen. When the water is low in oxygen, it will give carbon dioxide to the air in exchange for fresh oxygen, just as too much oxygen is surrendered to the air for more carbon dioxide. The point at which this balance is reached is called "100 percent saturation." (See Figure 8.) In this condition you will normally find your water, when colder than 70 degrees. Water clarity can also be a factor, because silt, plankton and foreign particles compete for space with dissolved oxygen.

Seasonal Changes. Just before ice-out on a northern lake, the oxygen content may be something like 3 to 4 ppm. It's this low because for three or four months the ice had acted as a lid, sealing the water off from the air and sunlight. Normally, this is sufficient oxygen for bass, due to their greatly reduced activity brought about by the cold water. Three to 4 ppm in summertime temperatures, of course, would spell trouble.

Once the ice breaks and winds kick up, water and air renew their acquaintance, setting out immediately to balance the scales. Since the ratio is so poor and the water so cold, the initial gas exchange is rapid. In just a day or two, depending on the strength of the wind, the entire lake should achieve a uniform oxygen content of a least 7 to 8 ppm. Then oxygen is no longer a concern, to the bass or us, and shouldn't be for at least another few months.

No two lakes are exactly the same, but in most of America's waters oxygen can become a problem in the warmer months. One reason is that since water thermally layers out (stratifies) during summer, the warmer, wind-mixed upper layers tend to seal off the lower, colder regions much like the ice did to the whole lake during winter. So, once fish and other organisms

23

exhaust the oxygen down deep, there's no way to replenish it. Limnologists have names for both these regions, but we are mainly interested in where they meet. That exact depth is called the "compensation level." Above it the oxygen supply can be replenished by wind-produced currents and the sun-loving plankton. Below it the waters are dark, dead and temporarily unreplenishable. (See Figure 10.) Theoretically, the poorer your lake's average water clarity, the shallower you'll find the compensation level and therefore the more oxygen stress the bass must endure.

The other reason oxygen can be a problem in summer comes from the ironic fact that the warmer the water, the more oxygen bass need, yet the less oxygen the water can hold. Back on Figure 8, notice where the 100 per cent saturation line intersects the one showing the amount of oxygen a five-pound bass requires for full activity. It occurs at approximately 8½ ppm for oxygen and 73 degrees for temperature. This means 73-degree water can hold roughly 8½ ppm, which is also the minimal amount a big bass needs for full feeding activity. In short, things are okay.

To the right on the chart, you see that as the temperature rises, not only does the bass' oxygen requirement increase, but the amount of oxygen water can hold decreases. If, for example, the water temperature is 75 degrees and in perfect oxygen balance with the air, a five-pounder will be unable to reach a full feeding state. As summer progresses and the water warms further, this condition invariably worsens and becomes one of the major reasons for the fishing slow-down of July and August in many waters.

Oxygen Maximums. While the gas exchange between water and air is slow, the rate at which plankton produce and destroy oxygen is not. During the sunlight hours, these little green gremlins crank out dissolved oxygen much faster than the water can pass it off to the air. This often creates pockets and layers of oxygen-rich water called "maximums." Baitfish and bass are drawn frequently to these maximums, forming a

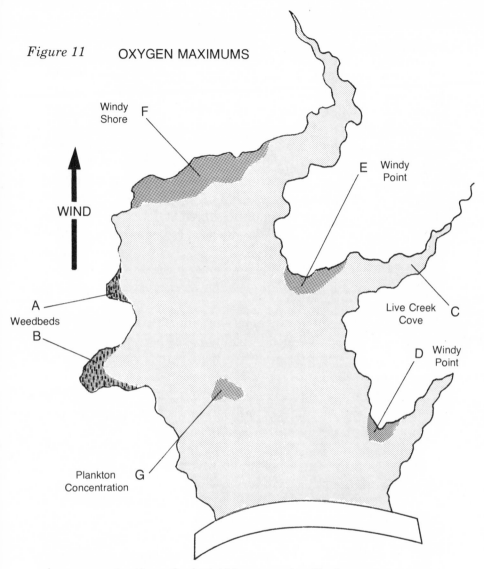

Figure 11   OXYGEN MAXIMUMS

Windy Shore   F

WIND

E   Windy Point

A

Weedbeds

B

Live Creek Cove   C

D   Windy Point

Plankton Concentration   G

nice concentration of what this game is all about.

By definition, maximums are areas where the oxygen content is higher than the surrounding water. In theory, then, 5 ppm could be a maximum if the rest of the water held only 4 ppm. Since a host of variables dictate the location and quality of a maximum, the easiest and fastest way to find one is with an oxygen monitor. Figure 11 shows a few places to start looking.

"A" and "B" represent weedbeds, where large concentrations of oxygen-producing plankton often occur. The weeds themselves also generate oxygen, but some scientists feel these are only "bubbles," not the dissolved variety that fish breathe. "C" shows a cove fed by a creek with running water. In the time it takes fallen rain to flow from the watershed to the lake, it can pick up extra oxygen from the air. "D" and"E" and"F" would be worth checking on windy days — in this case a south wind. Surface waters can pick up a little extra oxygen from the air, as they are carried across the lake by waves, then even more when they crash against the shore. And finally, out in the middle of nowhere is "G". This represents a maximum formed by a concentration of plankton, with no rhyme or reason for its presence. They drift with the wind and currents, and are where you find them. Shad sometimes hang within. And the bass are right below.

It should be pointed out, however, that in the cases of live creeks and windy shorelines, clean water and hard lake bottoms are a must. If, for example, a good rain is washing half of some farmer's field into the lake, those live-creek coves will be choked with silt, and therefore low in oxygen. And in the same manner, a loose, muddy bottom will be stirred up by crashing waves and a heavy undertow.

Looking at oxygen vertically, you'll find that it almost always "layers out" during summer, much the same as temperature. The highest ppm is usually at the surface, then steadily it decreases with depth. (See Figure 10.) Every now and then, in isolated sections of certain large bodies of water, you may find a pocket of high oxygen underneath layers of poor oxygen. This phenomenon is called an "oxygen inversion" and is rather rare. I went looking for one once, and my wife had to put out a "missing persons" on me.

The Oxycline. While the "compensation level" is the dividing line between "live" and "dead" water, the "oxycline" simply marks the last depth having enough oxygen to support bass while resting. It is also found with an oxygen monitor by taking readings from the surface to the bottom. When the ppm drops below 6 in normal summertime water temperatures, this will be the "oxycline" and it's unlikely any bass will be found deeper.

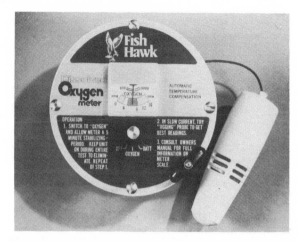

Fishhawk Oxygen Monitor

DO YOU NEED AN OXYGEN MONITOR?

If you have any question about your lake's oxygen condition during the summer, ask your local fisheries biologists. They usually keep tabs on such things and will be more than happy to tell you. If this isn't possible, borrow a friend's monitor some hot, calm day, then anchor over a deep part of the lake. With an electronic thermometer first locate the depth of your bass' ideal temperature. Then lower the oxygen probe to that exact depth and note the reading.

As a rule of thumb, if it's 6 ppm or less, an oxygen monitor would be well worth the investment. Six ppm is marginal, and the chances are the condition will worsen. If, instead, you find 8 ppm or better, lower the probe even further, watching the meter all the way. Should the oxygen drop to or below 6 ppm within the next five feet, again an oxygen monitor would probably be worth buying. For one thing, the compensation level tends to creep upward as summer wears on. Depending on the

weather, it may be only a couple days before it reaches the bass'
ideal temperature layer and forces him shallower. And even if
this didn't happen, it may next year. Or it may already be in
progress at other lakes you fish.

Even without an oxygen monitor, it's possible to detect a
potential oxygen problem. The most obvious clue is the water's
clarity. If you cannot see a lure more than a foot or two below
the surface, become suspicious. As we saw earlier, most of a
lake's summer oxygen comes from plankton, which need sunlight to produce it. So, if the water is murky, the sun's penetration will be limited to the upper extremes and so will the "good"
oxygen. Lakes with agricultural runoff are normally the most
susceptible to this dirty-water condition.

Sheltered lakes and ponds, even with clear water, often show
poor oxygen in the depths. Wind may not supply much oxygen
to water during summer, but it is responsible for creating
currents, which carry the plankton's oxygen to the darker

*Undaunted by bright light, this six-pounder hangs casually
above good cover in three feet of water. Theoretically, a non-
spawning bass in this position will be in at least a semi-positive
feeding mood.*

regions. Block out the wind, and only the upper, well-lighted depths will enjoy the luxury of good oxygen.

In a nutshell, if your favorite bassing hole is a cold, clear glacier lake, such as those in our northernmost states, a spring-fed quarry or a moderately clear shallow lake or pond that's exposed to the winds, chances are an oxygen monitor would not be worth the money. In any other waters, buy one — even if your wife has to get a second job to pay for it. You won't use it much from fall to late spring, but during summer it can pay off in big bass dividends.

SUMMARY

The minimum amount of oxygen required for a bass to be completely comfortable ranges from roughly 3 ppm to 10 ppm. It all depends on his size, his present state of activity and the temperature of the water he is in. For example, a five-pound largemouth resting in 40-degree water needs only 3 ppm to breathe without stress. On the other extreme, that same bass feeding actively in 85-degree water would need at least 10 ppm.

Water obtains the vast majority of its oxygen from microscopic plants called "plankton." If these organisms are not in abundance, such as during the cooler months, then the air is the contributor — only at a much slower rate. Water and air constantly try to stay balanced in oxygen with each other. When water is holding all the oxygen it can without passing some off to the air, it is said to be in a state of 100 percent saturation. Water clarity is important in how well oxygenated a body of water is, since plankton, silt particles and other minute objects compete with dissolved oxygen for space. Consequently, murky waters are the most susceptible to oxygen problems, especially when their temperatures rise past 70 degrees.

Like clear water, cold water is capable of holding more oxygen. So, oxygen seldom needs to be considered as a variable until summer. Oxygen maximums (any area of water containing more oxygen than the surrounding water) sometimes occur around weedbeds on calm sunny days, where streams feed the lake after a rain, and along windy shores on cloudy days.

The compensation level distinguishes the upper half of a lake — where oxygen can be replenished by sun and wind — from the bottom half — where the oxygen steadily dwindles during summer. The oxycline is simply that last depth having enough oxygen to keep bass comfortable in a resting state.

While other variables, namely water temperature, are controlling factors — telling bass what to do and when to do it, oxygen is a limiting factor — telling them whether they can do it and to what degree. Once the oxygen content drops below their minimum requirement, bass will try to compensate by (in order): finding more oxygenated water, breathing faster, turning down their metabolisms, ceasing to feed, shutting off all non-vital bodily functions as if in a state of hibernation, and if all else fails, regurgitating their stomach contents. (Digesting food calls for a little extra oxygen intake.) At this point, if the water condition does not improve within a few hours, the bass will die.

Chapter 3
Light

I'd guess that if someone walked into a room filled with 100 bass fishermen and said, "Gentlemen, *light penetration* is the key to bass fishing," ten people would get up and leave, ten would yawn and slowly doze off, 70 would turn a polite and interested ear to him, two would applaud and the remaining eight would pelt him with nearby throwables.

The controversy and confusion surrounding light probably had its origin in the early 70's when some writer reported that "bass have no eyelids." By itself, this was just an interesting bit of trivia, but we were then told that it meant the bass' eye had no protection from the sun, and therefore the fish had to retreat to deeper, darker water during daylight. To prove this theory, it was explained that bass in aquariums would shrink from sudden illumination and that bass in one clear lake swam to greater depths when pursued by divers with bright floodlights. Meanwhile, the world was being presented with another scientific fishing aid — the light meter.

Unfortunately, the results left much to be desired. Bass

fishermen caught a very low percentage of their fish from the specific "light layer" prescribed by the instrument. There was also a slight discrepancy in the undeniable fact that bass often lounged in brightly lighted shallows, apparently unconcerned with their lack of eyelids. This was particularly obvious during the spawning season, when many bass stay shallow for weeks. A new conclusion was drawn by many disgruntled anglers: Sunlight has little or no effect on bass. And the sky was darkened by flying light meters.

This entire misunderstanding is unfortunate, because light *is* important in bass fishing. But before it can help an angler, it must be put into its proper perspective. Those who feel it means everything must come to realize that no one variable is always the most important. Each takes its turn, depending on the lake's location, content, clarity and time of year. Those thinking it means nothing should look at a few facts with an open mind. Many of these facts are coming up, and I think they'll prove enlightening (pun intended).

THE EYE OF THE BASS

To begin with, bass can see in bright, natural light. It doesn't hurt their eyes. Yes, they do lack eyelids; and yes, they do have fixed pupils. A pupil is the circular opening in front of the lens. Ours open and close to changing light intensities, the bass' do not. But eyelids are primarily for keeping eyes moist and free from debris, not for shielding them from light. So whether bass have them or not makes little difference. And the same holds true for pupils. Just because theirs are fixed is no reason to believe they are ill-equipped in the area of light regulation. As a matter of fact, in many ways, their ocular system makes ours look like a dime store camera.

One method of light control is found in the retina. In much the same manner as our own, light enters the bass' eye through the lens, where it is focused into an image, then sent to the back of the eye and displayed upon the retina. Here, scattered all

32

over, are two types of light sensors called *rods* and *cones*. When the light striking the retina is brighter than what we would call room light, the cones — or color receptors as they are sometimes known — push outward to receive it. When the light is dimmer, the cones shrink back and the rods pop out. Rods are many times more sensitive to light than cones, but the images they send to the brain are only in black and white, and the various shades of gray.

Another method is a chemical called *melanin*. When illumination is at a maximum, such as the bass being in the shallows under a bright sun, receding back into the retina may not provide enough protection for the sensitive rods. In this case, the eye would release the melanin chemical to coat the rods with a light-reducing film. I guess you could say this safeguard is like having built-in sunglasses.

Also, there's strong speculation that bass can regulate incoming light by the simple back and forth movement of their lenses. Without getting too technical, it seems that the iris elongates when the lens is pushed out to its maximum, and shrinks to a tiny opening when the lens is pulled all the way back. Of course, the smaller the opening in the iris (remember that this opening is the pupil), the less the incoming light, and vice versa. It seems the bass' pupils may not be so "fixed" after all.

So far we have been speaking about ways bass' eyes deal instantly with light changes. The final feature is a gradual adjustment their eyes go through automatically during every 24-hour cycle. And again it involves the rods and cones. A few hours before sundown, the color-sensitive cones slowly begin withdrawing back into the retina, as the super-sensitive rods begin emerging. By a few hours after dark, this transition is completed and the bass has full night vision. He can't perceive color, but his eyes now are approximately 30 times more susceptible to light. As dawn approaches, then, the process reverses, and by the time the sun spans the trees, our bass is back to full daytime vision.

Even though bass apparently see well in bright light, and have a night vision to rival any tomcat's, light is still a strong factor in influencing their behavior at times. Here is the rule: *The larger the bass, the more concerned with light he becomes anytime it exposes him to his enemies or his prey.* Like all creatures, bass need security and food. And anything that hampers their obtaining either will be avoided, if possible. Let's look at the two factors individually.

The Security Factor (Enemies). Adult bass have little fear of anything below the surface, and this grows truer with every pound they put on. But it's the complete opposite when they see the image or shadow of a terrestrial creature upon the water. You can prove it for yourself in an aquarium. Come in from the side and put your nose on the glass, make faces or even quick, threatening gestures. The bass will just look at you. He may even move in for a closer look, depending on his level of amusement. But show your face, hand or any object directly above the aquarium and he'll dart away. Instinct tells him the world above is the home of his enemies.

Logically, then, bass find security in deep water. They like its lower light levels plus the distance it puts between them and the bad guys. They'd possibly stay there forever, too, if it weren't for one thing: They need food, and just about all of that commodity is found in the shallows. Caught between the devil and the beep blue sea? Not really. Deep water is not the bass' only source of security. In fact, I believe it's not even its best. Good cover is, even in only one foot of water. A thick bunch of weeds or brush in the shallows enables a bass to hide from his enemies and stay concealed from his prey at the same time. You can test this for yourself. The next time you catch a good bass off shallow cover, take him back to that spot (or similar nearby cover) and release him on the deep water side. If he's close enough to see the cover, he'll usually scoot right for it. If he isn't, then of course he'll dig for the depths.

Underwater telemetry is also bearing out cover's importance. Tiny transmitters surgically implanted in bass trace their daily and seasonal movements by radio. These studies are showing that a surprising percentage of bass in lakes with decent cover spend most of their time in the shallows, either taking up residence near a good structure or bouncing from one to the next. About the only time they see deep water is when threatened by imminent danger, during winter when the shallows are colder or during summer if the shallows get too warm. Take away all the cover and you would probably see a general shift to deeper water by most adult bass.

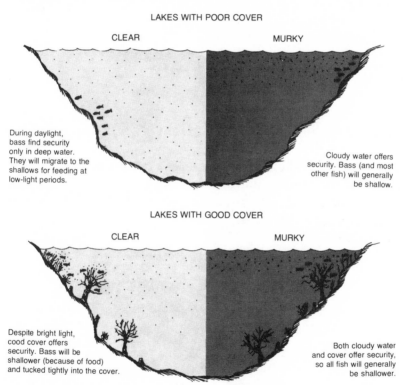

LAKES WITH POOR COVER

CLEAR   MURKY

During daylight, bass find security only in deep water. They will migrate to the shallows for feeding at low-light periods.

Cloudy water offers security. Bass (and most other fish) will generally be shallow.

LAKES WITH GOOD COVER

CLEAR   MURKY

Despite bright light, cood cover offers security. Bass will be shallower (because of food) and tucked tightly into the cover.

Both cloudy water and cover offer security, so all fish will generally be shallower.

Figure 12. Where Bass Find Security in Different Lake Types. With other variables being equal, the home of the bass will be at the shallowest depth offering concealment.

In lakes short on cover, bass still do not stay deep. They can find security in the shallows anytime the light level is low. In murky waters this is always. Even when the sun is high and brilliant, light penetration is minimal. Bass will come shallow, because they feel their enemies cannot see them, and stay there because of the abundance of food. In clear, coverless waters they may stay in the deeper, darker depths during the day, but will find safety and concealment topside from dusk to dawn or possibly under heavy overcasts. Daily vertical feeding migrations are common in lakes of this nature. And while they usually occur at night for big bass, a few may brave the shallows now and then during the day. The problem with catching them is that they can see you coming a long way off and may bore for the depths before the first cast. Solutions to this are discussed in Chapter Eight.

THE PREY FACTOR

For bass up to the fry stage, sunlight is a blessing. It protects them somewhat from larger predators and helps produce plankton, one of their sources of food. For bass in the 8-13-inch range, it's neither a hindrance nor help. But most adult bass over two pounds dislike high intensities of light because concealment is the best feeding strategy they have.

> *Minnow is nimble, minnow is quick.*
> *If bass gonna git you, he must hide by a stick.*
>
> (Anonymous — for good reasons)

Large bass can run down baitfish, but unless the pursuit lasts only a second, or the victim is of good size, the energy expended may surpass the energy gained. That could soon become lethal. So, bass like to hide out of sight, out of mind, ambushing unsuspecting niblets as they swim by. One way, of course, is by slipping just inside good cover, such as weeds or

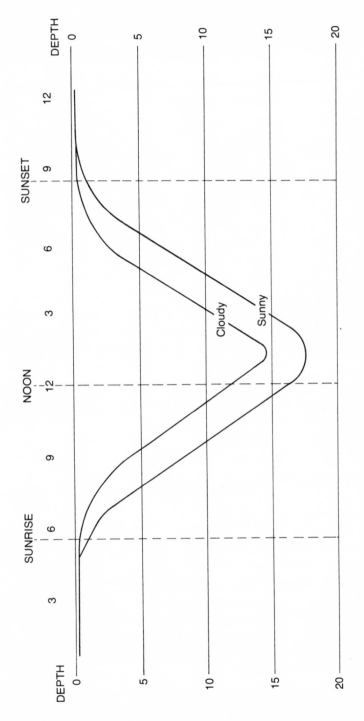

Figure 13. Depth at Which Zero Light Penetration Occurs. A fisherman's light meter which registers zero percent at approximately one foot-candle (dim room light) was used to demonstrate light penetration over a 24-hour period on an average lake in early summer.

37

the roots of trees. But even here some foodfish will see the bass shooting out at the last split second and make good their escape.

Many bass have learned to increase their odds of success by waiting until they gain the visual edge over their dinner. This occurs each day during the low-light period from dusk to dawn. (See Figure 14.) Most of what a bass eats — shad, minnows, crayfish — have poorly developed eyes. They cannot regulate the amount of light coming in and are painfully lacking in night vision. In anything less than normal daylight they are virtually blind. So while the sun is on this side of the horizons, it's a visual standoff between eater and eatee. But come the darker hours, the advantage swings strongly in favor of the bass. Granted, he may not see as well as he did during daylight, but his vision is still far superior to that of the baitfish.

Figure 14 compares the bass and his prey's ability to see during a typical 24-hour period. Beginning right at midnight, we find that neither can see particularly well, because the sun is doing its thing over the other side of the world. Still, the bass' night vision is on full tilt, so he has the definite edge. Then, about 2 a.m., his eyes begin changing over to day vision. His edge narrows steadily in the next hours, becoming only fair right before first light.

As the eastern sky brightens, the bass' visual advantage over smaller fish skyrockets. With some of his night vision still remaining, the low light of dawn is all he needs, while the prey's ability to see must wait for the gradual increase of the sun's angle. The first hour or so after sunrise is one of the two periods when the bass' visual edge is the greatest.

By late morning the sun is bright enough to afford full vision to both in the shallows. Then, in the late afternoon, the whole procedure starts over again, this time in reverse. Here, despite the fading light, the bass' ability to see remains high, because his eyes now are becoming more sensitive in anticipation of night's approach. The period just before sunset is the other in which the edge is the greatest. Then it is quickly lost right at

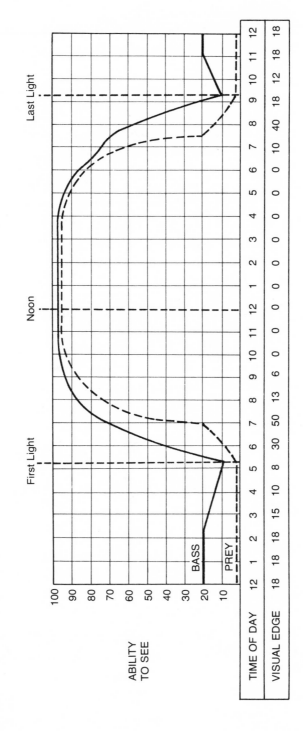

Figure 14

39

dark, but slowly rebounds as his eyes complete the transition to night vision.

WATER CLARITY AND VISIBILITY

The visual edge factor pertains only to waters with reasonable clarity or better. In clear lakes it becomes very important. In dirty water the whole principle blows up in our faces. The reasons are obvious. An excess of suspended particles (silt, algae, etc.) not only blocks out sunlight, it cuts down on the distance a fish can see. If it reaches a point where you cannot see a lure more than a foot under the surface, you can forget the visual edge factor. In fact, the bass may feed very little until the water clears up, assuming dirty water is not a normal year-round condition. In such a case, light could be scratched off your list of important variables altogether.

But, as a rule, poor clarity is only temporary. Since the condition was probably brought on by heavy rains upon a watershed of loose topsoil, as in an agricultural region, eventually the silt will settle to the bottom and normal clarity will return. Many lakes, ponds, rivers and backwaters of the United States experience frequent clarity fluctuations. In each case the current condition of the water may play a part in locating bass. It definitely will in determining when they feed. (See Chapter 10.)

WATER CLARITY AND THE BASS' LOCATION

Because of the larger bass' love affair with objects, where he positions himself in regard to them can be affected by differences in water clarity. For example, in clear water a resting bass can hang many feet from an object and still relate to it. A resting bass is not highly concerned with concealment, so he needs to be no closer to a structure than just to see it. If you wanted to bring your lure right past his nose — as you often must do with bass in this situation — you would have to make many casts on, around and above the object. However, since the bass could see your lure at a distance, you could work it fairly

MURKY WATER

CLEAR WATER

Figure 15. Bass resting in deep water are usually schooled and seldom aggressive, so your lure should come right to them. In murky water, bass hang close to their reference point because of limited visibility. Bumping your lure a few times off the structure should tell if they are interested. In clear water, the bass may be some distance above or to the side of the structure, so several scattered casts may be necessary.

fast. The reverse is true in turbid water. The poor visibility would force him to stay very near the object, so just a couple slow retrieves bumping directly over it should be enough.

Conversely, how a big bass relates to cover while feeding in the shallows is virtually the same, regardless of the water's clarity. He's either in or right against cover, lying in ambush. But water clarity does play a large part in just how shallow he decides to feed. As a rule, the poorer the visibility, the shallower he will come. First of all, turbid water makes bass less fearful of their enemies. Perhaps they know instinctively that if they can't see us, we can't see them. Secondly, in murky water the baitfish also move shallower because their food (plankton) may be non-existent in the sunless depths. And finally, since turbid water means poor lateral visibility, a bass may find it advantageous to be nearer the surface where he can better see food silhouetted against its light.

You can roughly determine the distance a bass can see with a simple formula. Using a fisherman's light meter, locate the first depth registering zero percent light penetration. Then divide it by six. If, for example, zero percent occurred at 18 feet, divide 18 by 6 and you come up with three. This would mean a bass could see a distance of approximately three feet laterally. When he looks up, however, the range will at least double because an object would be silhouetted against the bright surface. And when he looks down, visibility may drop a foot, if the background is dark. Another way to measure, although less accurate, is simply to lower a dark object into the water until it disappears. That distance will be roughly how far a bass can see laterally.

SUMMARY

Bright light does not hurt or blind the eye of the bass. Rather, it threatens their security, inducing them to hide from their enemies (namely us) by either tucking into good cover or going into deeper water. And, it exposes them to their prey, which they overcome by ambushing from good cover and/or by waiting until the low-light periods when they can see much better than their optically-poor lunch.

If you cannot see a white lure more than one foot beneath the surface, light will not be a factor in your angling strategy. In clearer water it will help determine how closely they relate to objects while resting, and when they will feed. In water with little or no cover, light will be a strong influence on the bass' preferred depth, but only if water temperature and oxygen are not factors.

Prof. Bruce W. Menzel and a graduate assistant at Iowa State University track largemouths via underwater telemetry. A tiny radio transmitter implanted inside the bass sends out a continuous signal which is picked up by a hydrophone held just under the surface. The "beeps" tell the biologists not only the bass' exact location, but the water temperature as well.

43

Chapter 4
Food

If bass fished for us, they would hang around kitchens and restaurants. It's here that we all congregate two or three times a day, stuffing food into open, trusting mouths. Imagine our vulnerability to a 1/0 hook buried in a pepperoni pizza.

The most successful bass fishermen approach their sport on the same principle: Rather than haphazardly searching for bass, they first locate those things which attract bass in large numbers. One of the most important is food. A high concentration of baitfish, crayfish or similar delectable morsels always draws and holds bass for as long as it lasts. Like any other life form, if the bass is to flourish, his amount of energy brought in must exceed the amount burned up.Since his world is hundreds of times more dense than ours, it doesn't take much moving around to burn up a few minnows worth of energy. That's why it is vitally important that a bass stay close to as much food as possible.

Like all the other variables, the more you understand about his food, the better your chances of outsmarting Mr. Mouth.

You should know what type of creatures he prefers to eat, which species are in your water at various times of the year, which he is feeding on at any given time, and the clincher — exactly where this food is found.

THE FOOD OF THE BASS

You may have read somewhere about the various forms of life found in the stomachs of adult bass — everything from beetles to baby ducks. These accounts are simply collections of exceptions. While bass in general may feed on many things in the course of a year, at any one moment they are probably being quite selective. Most fishermen find the bass' current priorities by trial and error. A lure is given so many chances, then retired and replaced by another until contact is made. It can be much to your advantage, however, if the first few lures you try are selected on the basis of what the bass want, not what appeals to you. This may sound insultingly obvious, but by being honest with yourself for a minute, you'll discover that over 90 percent of the lures in your tackle box were purchased because they hooked you. Force yourself to start each outing with something that imitates a favorite food of the bass, then keep returning to it periodically, even if a few bass have been caught on something altogether different.

Of course, it's impossible to tell you exactly what species of bass food are available in your waters. But this can be discovered easily by checking with local conservation officials or other knowledgeable fishermen. I would also recommend a slow walk or float along the shoreline, occasionally poking weedbeds and turning up stones to see what scoots away. I strongly promote returning all caught bass to the water, but if you do clean some, be certain to examine their stomach contents. The conservationist's way is to look into a freshly-taken fish's stomach with a funnel and flashlight before throwing it back. Once you know what your bass are feeding on, you can match lure color, size and action accordingly.

By and large, there are two primary entrees on the adult

largemouth's menu: the bottom-dwelling crayfish and the free-swimming baitfish such as shad, young gamefish and various minnows. Literally hundreds of species make up this latter group, but since they all share basically the same behavioral patterns we can lump them together for the sake of simplicity.

The Crayfish. There could be a number of reasons why crayfish are so popular with bass. One certainly is the high nutritional value they offer. Another is their perennial availability in so many of our lakes, ponds and rivers. And their ease of capture by the bass must also be taken into consideration. A crayfish is a short-burst swimmer with about as much speed and stamina as a beached whale. Add poor eyesight and it totals easy pickings — a bass has to expend very little energy for an exceptionally healthy meal. Finding out if your waters have these crustaceans is well worth the small effort.

It varies with the different species, waters and locations, but when water temperatures are below 50 degrees, most crayfish are burrowed deeply into the bottom hibernating. Bass apparently can't dig them out, so they turn their sights to other prey. Once the water warms, the crayfish pop back into the land of the swimming, preferring areas of small rocks or weedbeds, where they find both food and cover. With a fluttering of fuzz-like follicles just below their mouths, they can tease live minnows into range of their pincers, or they can simply filter plankton from the water with the same follicles.

They may feed at any time, but with the vulnerability their poor eyesight affords in daylight, they prefer the cover of darkness. Bass feed on them heaviest during summer, because at no other time are they more abundant. A good rock-bed will often be pulsating with crayfish, and the wisest old bass lays early claim to it, since all he needs to do is flip over a stone and zap the fleeing meal. A bass with a raw lower lip is undoubtedly doing just that. As the supply dwindles in the following months, so will the bass' preference for crayfish.

The Baitfish. Next in food value come certain baitfish. Recent studies are showing that small gamefish like bluegills are fairly low on the nutritional list, while shad and edible-sized bullheads rank at the top. Due to this, stocking lakes and ponds with them is becoming a common practice. Bullheads are bottom-feeders, not much different from crayfish in what they eat and how well they see. Very few studies have been done on these ugly things, but it's logical to assume they also prefer nighttime for the majority of feeding. Again, a fairly easy yet nutritional prey for bass.

The same is true for shad, only they add the extra benefit of achieving and then maintaining a high population, thus providing bass with a year-round food supply. Unlike bullheads, shad are school fish, even in the adult stage. And rather than work the bottom, they freely roam the upper layers, feeding entirely on plankton. At night they crowd into thick cover (weeds are ideal) and cease activity. At times, bass may organize a search and destroy mission after hours, sending a couple to crash into the sleeping schools, while the others hang on the rim, waiting to spear the isolated and confused. During the day, bass up to two or three pounds may follow shad schools around the lake. But most, particularly the lunkers, will wait for them in ambush or join in when some get cornered in the back of a cove or against the weedline.

In waters with few weeds or dense brush, shad may go deep at night and periodically during the day. This is usually out in the middle of the lake, away from bass-type structures. When such a school is found on your locator, you will probably see bass or other predators hanging above them. Unfortunately, these are very difficult to catch. Once the school or part of it comes back to the surface to feed on plankton, the bass may get beneath them to also resume feeding. Now they are more catchable.

FINDING THE FOOD

Just about everything a bass eats makes its home in the shallows. In fact, the closer he comes to the surface, the more variety and quantity he normally finds. The problem with terms like "shallows" is that they are ambiguous. What's shallow for one man on his lake may be deep for another on his. It all depends on the particular time and type of water being fished, plus of course each man's definition of the term. So you and this book will be on the same wavelength, from here on "shallow water" will be defined as "that layer of water beginning at the surface and ending at that depth where most of the lake's food ends." Deep water then is simply any water below this.

In one lake the shallows may end at 20 feet, while in another perhaps only a few miles away it may be just five feet. This is why it's important to know how to find that exact depth where shallow water changes to deep water on any lake at any time. Bass found above this depth will more than likely be feeding. And that requires certain tactics on your part. Those found below it will be resting, calling for a different approach altogether.

Light Penetration. One key lies in light penetration— how deeply sunlight enters the water before its life-giving rays are filtered out. From the standpoint of light, most bodies of water are divided into two main regions. Each has an impressive scientific name, but for our purpose the "lighted region" and "dark region" will suffice. The former could also be called the "living region" because it's here that microscopic organisms known as plankton find the proper amount of sunlight on which to thrive. When the sun strikes these little green fellows, they draw nutrients and carbon dioxide from the water, using them to grow, manufacture oxygen and reproduce. If the light is not intense enough, such as in the dark region, they cannot. (See Figure 16.)

The Food's Food. In bass fishing a study of plankton is much more important than many people realize. It's any body of water's bread of life—in one way or another every living thing must have it to survive. Shad, for example feed on plank-

48

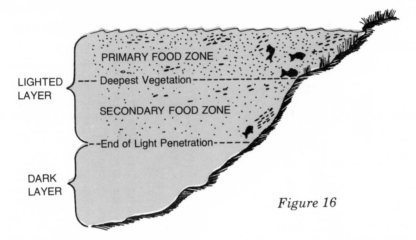

Figure 16

Lighted Layer – Enough sunlight to sustain plankton, registering 100% on a fisherman's light meter.
Primary Food Zone – From the surface to the last depth having rooted vegetation. Weeds are cover for baitfish, so most of them, and feeding bass, are found here.
Secondary Food Zone – Contains plankton, but without weeds baitfish will be scarce unless brush is abundant. A few bass may feed here.
Dark Layer – Too little light for plankton, registering anything less than 100% on the light meter. Even if oxygen is good, bass will feed little here since lack of plankton means lack of baitfish.

ton exclusively, as do most minnows and fry. When crayfish aren't eating it directly, they are preying on the various small life forms that do. So, where there is proper sunlight in the water, there will be plankton. And where there is plankton in large quantities, there will probably be crayfish and baitfish, which should signal the presence of bass.

Plankton is not scattered evenly throughout the lighted region however. Greater densities will be found "trapped" in weedbeds, or stacked against windy shores. During summer stratification, those layers of water hosting a temperature in the ideal range of plankton (72-75 degrees) plus adequate sunlight will often experience "blooms."

Even a high concentration of plankton does not guarantee

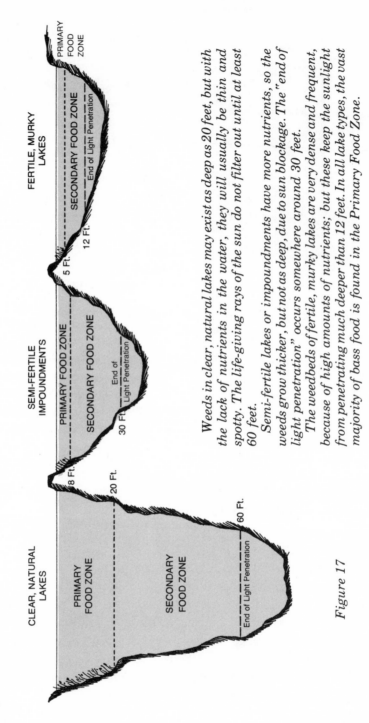

Weeds in clear, natural lakes may exist as deep as 20 feet, but with the lack of nutrients in the water, they will usually be thin and spotty. The life-giving rays of the sun do not filter out until at least 60 feet.

Semi-fertile lakes or impoundments have more nutrients, so the weeds grow thicker, but not as deep, due to sun blockage. The "end of light penetration" occurs somewhere around 30 feet.

The weedbeds of fertile, murky lakes are very dense and frequent, because of high amounts of nutrients; but these keep the sunlight from penetrating much deeper than 12 feet. In all lake types, the vast majority of bass food is found in the Primary Food Zone.

Figure 17

50

the presence of crayfish or baitfish. Just like bass, they need security and protection. So they, too, utilize cover. And those objects or irregularities that offer the most to the most will be the strongest crayfish-baitfish magnets. Examples would be large dense brushpiles, broad rocky areas and thick weedbeds. Since the latter is probably the best and is found in most waters, let's take a look at where you'll usually find them growing.

Again, light penetration is the main factor. Like plankton, weeds require sunlight to exist. But the intensity must be far greater. If you'll look again at Figure 16, you'll see that rooted vegetation cannot grow as deeply as plankton for this reason. Consequently, the lighted region is divided into the "primary food zone" and the "secondary food zone." The separator is the depth of deepest vegetation. Above this line baitfish find both food and cover. Below it there is only food, unless dense brushpiles and rocky areas are present. So, in most of our lakes and ponds (those having weeds) the vast majority of baitfish and crayfish will be found in the primary food zone, which runs from the surface down to the last depth having rooted vegetation. If, on the other hand, your water is weedless, the primary will go as deeply as good brushpiles or rockbeds do within the lighted region, and probably be less definable. In "dishpan" ponds and lakes with virtually no cover it will probably extend all the way down to the bottom of the lighted region, eliminating the secondary food zone altogether.

It's really quite easy to find the primary food zone in your waters, and it's one of the smartest things you can do. A lure running through it will be looking for scattered, more aggressive bass tucked tightly into good cover, if present. One running below it should be seeking bass of a more lethargic mood hanging loosely near structure, and possibly schooled.

HOW WEEDLINES VARY IN DIFFERENT WATERS

In any body of water the depth at which weeds grow and their thickness depend largely on the water's clarity. (See Figure

17.) A natural glacier-formed lake, such as found in Minnesota and Wisconsin, will often have weeds growing as deep as 20 feet. Being fed mostly by springs, rather than land runoff, the water stays beautifully clear, allowing sunlight to penetrate a long way down. But clear water normally signals a lack of fertility (nutrients) and that means both plankton and weeds will be minimal. The weeds may grow down to 20 feet and the plankton to 60 feet, but they will be thin and spotty.

On the other extreme are the fertile murky lakes found predominantly in agricultural areas. A lack of nutrients in this water is never a problem, thanks to the ample supply washed in from farmers' fields during heavy rain. Weeds seldom grow much deeper than five feet in these waters, because the sunlight is quickly filtered out. But what the vegetation lacks in area, it makes up for in density.

Between these two types are the majority of our bass waters, like the man-made impoundments. Here the water clarity may fluctuate greatly over the course of a year, but on the average the sunlight is intense enough to maintain weeds no deeper than 8-10 feet. Compared to the fertile murky waters just discussed — which often have a thick green ring around the entire perimeter and a light penetration of about 12 feet — these semi-fertile lakes support most of their vegetation in the upstream ends where more nutrients have piled up. The lower ends near the dam are usually too steep and rocky to catch and build up silt for weed growth, but you can still find some "greens" in the backs of coves. On the average, the end of light penetration occurs around 30 feet.

Let me quickly explain the criteria used to determine the end of light penetration. (For a more detailed explanation of light see Chapter Three.) The instrument I use is a typical fisherman's light meter which measures light in percentages from zero to 100. (A picture of the Fishhawk 530 Temperature/Light Meter is shown at the end of Chapter One.) While the probe is being lowered, as long as the meter registers 100 percent light, it is in the lighted layer. The instant the needle drops below 100 percent, it has entered the end of light penetration. In other words, it's in the line between the lighted layer and the dark layer. This doesn't mean a bass can no longer see here, rather the life-giving rays of the sun have been filtered out to where plant life cannot be maintained. From my own tests with this light meter, I've found that one percent of light is roughly equal to one foot-candle — about half the illumination of ordinary room light. This is more than enough light for bass to see.

LIVE CREEK COVES

Many lakes and impoundments have coves fed by streams. These are usually better fish magnets, mainly because right after a rain it's like someone spilled a grocery truck. Everything from insects to nightcrawlers wash into the cove, providing a sudden banquet to any fish that cares to partake. Not only will bass feed on the incoming terrestrial life, but the foodfish attracted here as well. Live creek coves are better even when it's not raining, because the inflow often brings warmer water in the cooler months and cooler, more oxygenated water in the hotter months. However, bass normally avoid areas with too strong a current when the spawning season is on. Besides possibly washing away the eggs, it can smother them with the high content of silt such currents often carry in from land.

HOW MUCH BASS EAT

The factors regulating a bass' daily food consumption are innumerable, but there are a few rules of thumb. First, scientists figure a bass needs one percent of his body weight per day just to live, and three percent to grow normally. (Three percent of a four-pounder is equal to roughly 24 crayfish.) This applies only to the growing season when water temperatures are near his preferred 68-75 degrees and he can digest food in 12 to 18 hours. In 40-degree water, for example, digestion takes up to four days, so eating 24 crayfish or the equivalent a day would be impossible. The same holds true when the oxygen is poor, the water too hot or when once-clear water suddenly turns turbid. Rather than combat tough conditions for questionable results, bass will decrease activity and wait things out. If you find them not hitting for days on end this is probably why. For a long time it has been believed that late spring produces the best fishing because the bass are on their shallow-water beds and easier to get a lure to. The truth is that this is the one time of year when conditions are at their best — ideal water temperature, sufficient oxygen, hungry bass and a low food supply.

SUMMARY

Find out what exactly the bass in your waters are feeding on at any given time, then select lures that match it in color, action and size. Find the areas with the highest concentrations of plankton and cover. Light penetration determines the depth of plankton which baitfish feed on, which in turn brings the bass. Any depth reading 100 percent or better on a fisherman's light meter will probably support this green microscopic plant life. Weedbeds and windy shores often hold concentrations. Since the food of the bass — crayfish and baitfish — also require cover, locate those vast weedy brushy and rocky areas which lie within the lighted region (100 per cent light). If weeds are abundant, the major feeding layer of the bass will usually run from the last depth having rooted vegetation up to the surface. This layer is also called the primary food zone, or if you prefer, the shallows.

When a bass is in the shallows, he is probably feeding. Exceptions would be during the spawning season, during late summer when poor oxygen below forces him to stay, or when the lake has such good shallow-water cover that he spends even his non-feeding hours here. Being up and feeding means the bass are scattered, agressive and more vulnerable to lures. Below the primary food zone, they are considered to be in deep water and will generally be more schooled, less willing to hit and harder to locate. This transition depth can be anywhere

54

from three to 30 feet, depending on the lake's clarity and structure.

Except during the spawning season, coves with live feeder streams are the best, because of the food washed in after rains, the warmer water brought in during cold months and the cooler more oxygenated water during the hotter months.

Bass need one percent of their body weight for food intake daily to stay alive in ideal temperatures, and three percent to grow normally. Digestion in this temperature range takes 12 to 18 hours. In 40 degrees, it takes up to four days. A four pound bass must eat approximately 24 crayfish or the equivalent daily for normal growth in late spring to early fall. Bass often turn themselves off to wait out unfavorable conditions, such as the summertime tandem of hot water and low oxygen.

Today you can find a lure to match almost anything a bass may feed on. Here a Rebel Deep Wee-R mimics a shad.

Chapter 5
Structure and Other Variables

Because the purpose of Part One of this book is to deal factually and concisely with each of the more important variables, our discussion of "structure" will be relatively short. All you need to know about it can be covered in a few basic principles.

I am convinced you will become a better bass fisherman by studying structure from the viewpoint of the bass — exactly what they look for, what purposes structure must fulfill and its location.

Once you understand the underlying basics, you'll be more capable of finding the bass at any time in any water — and you'll do it much faster than if you trial-and-errored your way down a long, memorized list.

THE FOUNDATION OF STRUCTURE

For the uninitiated, we'll quickly define "structure." It is, quite simply, "submerged objects (trees, tires, weeds, etc.) and irregularities in the bottom contour (drop-offs, creek channels, where mud turns to rock, etc.) that bass relate to." In short, it's anything different from its surroundings.

Bass and most other fish use structure for two main purposes — for *cover* to hide from their prey and their enemies, and for *reference points* to keep themselves oriented. As a rule, bass seek the cover aspect only in the shallows. Here they encounter both prey and enemies. They use structure for reference points while resting in deeper water or moving from one place to another. These two uses are the foundation of understanding structure, and should be permanently stamped into your bass-seeking mind. Now let's look at each in more detail.

THE TWO ROLES OF STRUCTURE

REFERENCE POINTS	COVER
To keep bass oriented while resting in deep water, and traveling from one place to another.	To hide bass from prey and enemies while in the shallows.

Figure 18. Cover. Bigger bass are more fearful of things from the "world above" and rely heavily on ambush to catch prey, so they tuck into cover in the shallows. The less inhibited smaller bass run down their food, and are not as dependent on cover in the shallows. Reference Points. In deep water, bigger bass fear practically nothing so they hang lazily around objects. Smaller bass fear larger fish, so they hang nearer.

REFERENCE POINTS

Compared to other freshwater gamefish, largemouths prefer warmer water than most. But this does not necessarily mean they all live in the shallows. In fact, their fear of things from "the other world" is so ingrained, that if bass had their way, they'd stay in the security of deep water all their lives. This, of course, isn't possible because almost everything they eat is found in the upper layers, as are their spawning grounds. Even if the majority of your bass are caught from shallow water, remember that in general most of the time most of the bass are where they really prefer to be — in their deep-water resting areas. The largest exception to this is in bodies of water loaded with ideal cover. Even in the extreme shallows, good cover apparently provides all the security they need, so some bass just stay there all the time, going deeper only when forced by adverse conditions.

Sometimes called a "sanctuary" or the bass' "home," the outstanding feature of a deep-water resting area is the reference point. It doesn't really matter whether it's an object (such as a tree) or an irregularity (like a sudden drop-off) it just has to be some obvious feature the bass can hang around to stay oriented while resting and recognize when going to or coming from an excursion. If it also provides cover, fine, but that element is not usually necessary. The deep water serves as all the protection a bass feels he needs.

So, if bass use anything from boulders to beer cans as reference points, what makes them prefer one structure over another? Now we're getting to the secrets of finding the deep-water resting areas. First and probably foremost, *the closer the structure is to a good feeding area, the better.* This cannot be stressed enough. Bass, especially the old-timers, find very little thrill in swimming long distances everytime they wish to eat. The farther they travel, the more they must ingest to make up for the energy expended getting there. This isn't laziness, it's a matter of survival. Theoretically, then, a scrawny twig adjacent to a food-infested shallow area would serve as a better home than a large hollow log a mile away.

Next, this structure will be even more attractive to bass if it *is in sequence with other reference points leading to the feeding ground.* Such a series of structures creates a "highway" for the bass to follow going to and from the shallows. One interesting thing to remember is that the dirtier the water, the closer together these should be. When a bass is at one structure, he prefers being able to see the next. In man-made impoundments old creek channels and roadbeds make excellent highways in any water clarity. In natural lakes, weedlines and narrow points are more the ticket.

Figure 19. The tree on the bank of the feeder stream is an ideal structure for the bass, being close to shallow feeding grounds and providing a "highway". Its largeness means it can hold more bass. The channel intersection is also good for the same reasons, but is further from the shallows and not as large. The lone tree may hold some bass, but lacks a well-defined highway. Any stump along the stream could hold one or two bass, and the nearer it is to the shallows, the better.

Once you find a good area, chances are it will contain a number of different structures, each meeting these two requirements. While they all are potential bass hangouts, usually your search can be narrowed to just a few. First of all, it's only logical that the *larger structures will harbor more bass*. A stump may be an excellent reference point, but because of its size it may support no more than one or two bass. Also, it would be harder for you to find. A big bushy tree, on the other hand, is easier to locate on a depth finder and can handle an entire school.

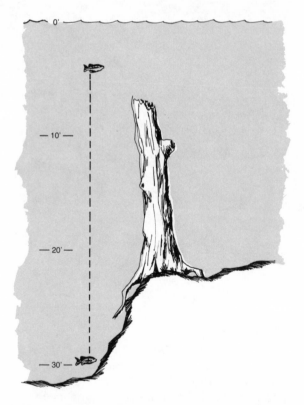

Figure 20. Tall structures are often perennial resting areas for bass, since as their preferred depth shifts up and down, they can move with it and still relate to the same reference point.

Bass also prefer *tall objects or irregularities.*Since their ideal depth often shifts up and down, a standing tree or steep rock bluff means the bass can shift right along with the changes and still keep relating to that same reference point. The taller structures are often perennial bass resting areas for just that reason.

COVER

Even though most of the time most of the bass are in deep water, those that are shallow are considerably more catchable. With the exceptions of spawning and being forced up by poor oxygen, a shallow bass is a feeding bass, and is therefore more apt to crunch a lure. There is definite merit in learning what largemouths demand from structure while visiting the shallows. As stated earlier, this is mainly cover, to conceal them from prey and enemies. And like deep-water reference points, just any old structure won't do.

Rule number one, of course, is that *the cover must be among food.* Bass just don't do well eating sticks and mud. They know what type of prey offers the most nutrition and they know where to find it. Usually it's around dense, fine-stemmed structures, like weeds and brushpiles. These provide the prey with protection from the bass. When threatened, the smaller fish can dart into the tiny openings where the larger predators can't follow. Vast rocky areas can also be good.

The second rule — less strict, but important nonetheless — is that *the cover should offer the bass good concealment.* His favorite tactic is ambushing, so he needs a spot where the prey has trouble seeing him, plus where a fast exit (to zap a minnow or run from danger) is possible. For example, the outer edge of a weedbed would fulfill both prerequisites whether the bass lie up against it to wait for something wandering out of the weeds, or lie just inside, ready to nail a victim swimming past. The same could hold true for a brushpile or the top end of a fallen tree. In any of these cases the cover blends in with the bass' natural coloration and makes him more difficult to see. The

61

other camouflage trick he uses is simply to hang in a shadow. As was explained in the chapter on Light, most prey types see well in normal bright light, but poorly in anything less. Therefore, something lurking in the shadow of a stump, log or big rock would go virtually unnoticed. One exception to this is when bass feed around rockbeds and rocky points. The crayfish and minnows they seek are usually obtained simply by uprooting the stones, so there is no need for concealment on the bass' part.

Finally, the better shallow-water ambushing locations will be *on or very near a major travel route of baitfish,* particularly in lakes where shad are the main food source. Roaming a lot during daytime, shad need highways just like bass, and they often take rest stops around various structures they encounter. The most obvious, most used and certainly the most common travel route is the shoreline. In lakes and ponds with heavy vegetation, it would be the weedline. In many larger impoundments, where weeds are not predominant, but flooded timber is, the treelines, brushlines and shallow creek channels run a close second to the shoreline. Keep in mind that the extreme shallows are the home of most baitfish. Although the lake may be laced with good-looking highways, most will be too deep to be used by the bass' food.

DEPTH FINDERS

For helping you locate structures, bottom depths and occasionally fish, there's only one hyphenated word in equipment — depth-finder. You can still catch bass without one, but you'll catch more with one. And you'll certainly have more fun. When the fishing slows, as it often does, you can still enjoy the sport by just motoring around, watching the red "bleeps and blurps" on the flasher's face tattle away the lake's secrets. Few things are as important as learning the bottom, and nothing can teach you like a good depth-finder.

Actually, the question today is not whether to buy one, it's whether to get the kind with a graph readout. It costs more and many anglers wonder if it's worth the money. I doubted it myself until I began field-testing a few models in 1974. Now I wouldn't give mine up for five minutes with Farrah. The best feature of all is that no matter how well you think you can read a regular flashing type depth-finder, one with a graph will make you better. It shows exactly what that last confusing melee of red flashes was, leaving practically nothing to your interpretation, which, as you will discover, is often less than accurate. In time you will become an accomplished flasher

Lowrance 610
Flasher-Graph
Depth-Finder

reader and can use the graph less frequently. (Graph paper costs about $6 per roll.)

Secondly, a graph readout serves as your memory. It can be constantly scouting the bottom, while your eyes stay on more important things, like a pontoon boat full of drunks about to beach on your deck. You need only check the readout occasionally to see if anything interesting was just passed over. Finally, it provides a permanent record that can be pulled out and studied at your convenience.

What model you buy is mostly a matter of personal choice and the amount you wish to spend. I'm partial to the Lowrance 610A Flasher/Graph, but probably because I've been using one for the past four years. It is accurate, well-built and offered at one of the most reasonable prices. There are other high-quality brands, so I suggest you see your local dealer.

Lowrance 515
Truline Recorder
Depth-Finder

OTHER IMPORTANT VARIABLES

The Pressure Variable. You received a phone call from Farmer McFoul, who ten years ago built a beautiful farm pond and stocked it with catfish, bluegills and bass. He never let anyone fish it and never did himself. Then suddenly it seemed he developed a craving for fried bass, but not knowing the first thing about catching them, he called you to come out and do it for him. Being the gentleman you are, you politely obliged — then hung up and burst into elated hysterics.

Our fantasy continues. The next day you came to the one-acre paradise just at sunup. Your first cast with a purple "Gotcha" fooled a six-pound bass. A few minutes later in came a four-pounder, then a three, and another three, then a two. The following two hours produced nothing, so you hauled your 18 pounds of bass up to old McFoul. Tickled pink, he said that you could fish his pond anytime. And you did, for the next five mornings, and caught nothing!

What did you do wrong?

Answer: You should never have come back after that first morning. You had taken almost every catchable bass.

Despite our optimistic imaginations, the bass supply in any body of water is not unlimited. Nor is it fully recharged year after year. As a matter of fact, fisheries biologists regard 25 pounds of bass per acre as a respectable population. Fifty pounds per acre is fabulous — and rare. Ten pounds is sadly common. So, the odds are that you wiped out most of the keeper bass in that pond for at least the next year. A few undoubtedly remained, but they would be that 10 to 30 percent that seldom fall for lures. Perhaps this is the Great Game Warden's way of insuring the preservation of species.

The pressure variable has become a very real thing in recent years, especially in bass fishing. Word leaks out that a particular lake is hot, and anglers swoop in like vultures to a dead mule. Studies have shown that within just weeks, sizeable waters can be fished out of bass. It all depends, of course, on the number of fishermen per acre of water. It's highly unlikely that our huge impoundments, like Bull Shoals or Texoma could ever be fished out completely, but the bass population can certainly drop at times to where most anglers lost interest.

Bass Per Hour. Before your first cast on any unfamiliar body of water you should have some idea of what to expect in the way of pounds and numbers of bass. If you go by what a brochure says, you may not be happy with anything less than a 50-pound stringer. In which case I offer you the best of luck and my biggest crying towel. On the other hand, if you have a realistic idea of what the average bass-per-hour take is on that water at that time of year, you can adjust your sights accordingly. That way, when day is done you will know whether you beat the lake or it beat you. The latter would probably mean the bass were simply uncooperative, but it could also suggest trying a different pattern.

It's impossible to say what the average catch rate is for every chunk of water in the country. But since many bass fishermen like to identify with the professionals, perhaps it would help you to know how they have done in the big national B.A.S.S. tournaments over the past 10 years. Five bass per hour? Seven? Ten? Would you believe roughly *three-tenths*! That's one keeper bass for every three hours of fishing. And these guys fish hard. Perhaps now you won't feel so bad when you bring in less than a poster catch.

The Sunday Syndrome. In defense of the professionals, however, it must be pointed out that in tournaments the pressure variable is at its worst. With over 200 anglers going all-out for six solid days, you can bet any given bass sees a number of lures sputter past his nose. In some areas of the lake it probably looks like a fashion show. All the commotion, plus steadily dwindling numbers of unhooked bass adds up to mighty tough fishing.

I call this the "Sunday syndrome" because any popular lake receives its most severe fishing pressure on weekends. If you have ever fished on both a weekday and a Sunday, you know your luck invariably will be better on the former. It seems the

bass are disturbed by all the attention they get on weekends and either turn off or move to quieter water. And with all the fishermen, there are fewer fish to go around. Too much pressure can disrupt normal patterns, so it must be considered an important variable.

The Weather Variable. Many changes in bass behavior can be linked to changes in water temperature, oxygen and/or light penetration. Variations in these are usually caused by weather. Though it seldom affects fish directly, weather does give us clues to past, present and future changes in Mr. Mouth's daily routine — specifically where he'll be and how willing he is to hit your lure.

For example, say it's spring, the water temperature is 50 degrees, the air is 45 degrees, the sky is cloudy for the first time in three days and the wind is brisk. Under these conditions you can expect tough fishing. Bass turn off when cold water turns colder, and that's exactly what it will do this day, thanks to the absence of a warming sun, plus the wind mixing cooler air into the water. Add the sun and you may find a few nice bass just under the surface in a wind-sheltered cove. Add 20 degrees to the air and the fishing could become pretty good throughout the lake, because the water temperature would be rising and thus stimulating the fish.

Now say it's early summer. The water is thermally stratified with the surface reading 75 degrees, the air is 80 degrees, the sky again is cloudy for the first time in three days and the wind just ripples the surface. Here you can expect good fishing. The key this time is the cloud cover, which can turn bass on by darkening the shallows and giving a greater sense of security, plus a slight visual edge over the prey. And the past few days being bright and sunny makes this all the better, as does the rippled surface scattering some of the sky's light back into the atmosphere. Here, water temperature has little to do with stimulating the bass, since it's already in their preferred range.

We won't go any deeper into weather's role here, because

other chapters, specifically Chapter Nine, cover it thoroughly. Just keep in mind that sun, wind, and air temperature, and how all three work together, are the keys to watch. Tomorrow's forecast can tell you a lot.

THE LAKE-TO-LAKE VARIABLES

Every time you set foot on a new body of water, it's a different ball game. Each has its own unique personality and you must try to analyze its secrets. Most of this is accomplished by studying the major variables covered in Part One — water temperature, oxygen, light penetration, structure and food conditions.

Following are a few more variables it never hurts to check out. Thanks to maps and Ma Bell, this can usually be done before you even see the water. Checking these may be a big factor in helping select new lakes.

Latitude. Obviously, lakes are generally warmer the farther south they are. A warmer "thermal history" means a higher "ideal temperature" for its bass. In Wisconsin they may prefer 68 degrees, in Texas 75. Sometime during summer, waters around and below the 40th parallel often become too warm in the shallows for bass, forcing them deeper and possibly making the fishing tougher. Southern waters mean longer growing seasons and therefore indicate larger bass, although fertility is also a factor. The colder the lake's thermal history, the later the fishing begins in the spring and the earlier it ends in the fall.

Surrounding Terrain. Sheltered lakes are normally warmer than open ones. The lack of wind mixing the water causes a more severe degree of thermal stratification in summer, meaning warmer shallows and cooler depths. Sheltered waters also suffer the likelihood of occasional oxygen problems, particularly if they are murky most of the time. At winter's end, open bodies of water will see the earliest bassing action since the wind takes the ice out sooner and stirs in more oxygen more quickly. As a rule, the steeper the terrain around a lake, the clearer the water will be and the deeper you will probably have to fish if ample shallow cover is not present.

Bottom Type. Since dark colors absorb and hold more heat, lakes with muddy bottoms will be warmer, especially if they are also shallow. Good weed growths signal good fish populations, but too many weeds can make fishing tedious. Bass seem to have more successful spawns in clean-bottomed water, and generally prefer this type of contour for their other activities. Better bass lakes nearly always have a pleasant balance of clean rocky bottoms and sufficient — but not overly so — weedbeds or brushpiles and flooded timber.

Age of the Lake. Older lakes can denote bigger bass. Good brush may not exist anymore, due to the deterioration effect of water, so stumps, logs and big rocks may be the main structures. All lakes, if left unmanaged, go through fishing cycles, peaking in bass populations roughly every tenth year. By finding out how the fishing has been in past years and the trend, you may have a good idea of what to expect on a particular lake this year.

THE "WHO-KNOWS" VARIABLES

The following variables earn this dubious classification because I have been unable to find enough scientific proof to either support their authenticity or expose their quackery. Nor have my own experiments and experiences produced anything conclusive. Still, some very good bass fishermen proclaim their validity and I myself have found them helpful at times. So, each deserves at least a consideration, keeping in mind, however, that what is said here is only my opinion.

Barometric Pressure. I believe a barometer can occasionally be an indicator of whether the bass have moved up or down, are feeding or not. But it's a poor one. Changes in air pressure are associated with changes in sky conditions, air temperature, humidity, and wind speed and direction, which in turn cause changes in water conditions, which in turn affect fish. If you really want to know what the bass are up to, look to the water. If you can't "see" the water, look to the weather. And if you can't "see" the weather, then poke an eyeball at the barometer.

Exactly what it will tell you about the bass' behavior is open to question. I monitored the barometric pressure hourly for two years and compared it with each fishing excursion. I found no consistency whatsoever. Others claim they have. But even these staunch believers disagree on what a barometer tells about bass, so I see no point in passing along suggestions, other than to test it for yourself in your part of the world.

The Moon. It's a fact that the moon's gravitational pull on the earth is responsible for tides, which affect fish movements in the ocean, seas and large lakes like Superior. The last time a tide rolled in on one of my favorite lakes or ponds I must have been asleep. I'm not disputing the possibility of some "power" radiating from the moon. In fact, I'm convinced there is. But until science uncovers what it is, then documents its direct effect on bass, my faith goes into the moon's most obvious characteristic — light at night. When it's high and full, or nearly so, it floods the water with enough illumination to make night feeding a lucrative proposition for bass and other predators with a keen night vision, especially in clear water.

It's interesting to note that most bass fishermen who follow moon phases live in Florida or other coastal areas of the southern U.S. With the moon being more directly overhead more of the time here, its gravitational effects are undoubtedly stronger, perhaps to the extent that they do act upon fish in inland waters. This could be further enhanced by the fact that these regions usually experience longer periods of consistent weather, thereby reducing weather's overriding influence as a fishing variable. In my region of the Midwest, for example, a new weather system moves in every three days virtually all year long. If the weather were not so predominant a variable here, perhaps the moon phases would be.

Solunar Periods. The Solunar Tables, based on the cycles of the sun and moon, forecast the times of day fish will be feeding.

My two-year study of these proved so disappointing that today I don't even check them. The vast majority of experts I've checked with feel the same. Like moon phases, the sun's relation to the moon probably does affect life on earth, especially the lower classes like fish. But there are factors which affect them far more. For example, I am of the strong opinion that the times a bass feeds each day are determined mostly by when he fed last, when his food becomes available and when water conditions such as light and temperature are the most favorable. These three — separate, together or in tandem with other stimuli — are so ever-present and dominant that a Solunar pattern has trouble getting established, let alone remain in most of this country's waters. But, again, I recommend testing Solunar Tables or any charted fishing times for yourself.

PART TWO
THE METHODS

Chapter 6
Body Temperature

The first time I tried taking a bass' temperature was in 1971. I was about to release a freshly taken four-pounder when the recently-read words came to mind: "You can take a fish's body temperature by shoving the probe of your electronic thermometer down its throat...next, lower the probe into the water until that same temperature is found...that depth will be from where your fish came, and therefore a good depth to look for others."

The logic of that maneuver was inescapable. Cackling sinisterly to myself, I pulled the reluctant bass back aboard and rammed the temperature probe into place. I got a reading of 77 degrees. I then lowered the probe into the water to find at what depth 77 occurred.

It didn't. In fact, the warmest I could find was 72 degrees, and that was at the immediate surface.

Since it was common knowledge that a fish's body will have the same temperature as the water surrounding it, the only conclusion I could draw was that this particular bass had been sunbathing on the beach. Thankful no one else had witnessed the episode, I quickly stuck that tactic where the sun never shines, as I'm sure many other bass anglers had also done.

Ironically, today I not only take the body temperature of almost every bass I catch, I consider it a highly valuable fish-finding technique! Why the change of mind? Because in the initial stages of researching this book, I discovered that I (and probably everyone else) had not been given the true facts about a fish's body temperature and which type of thermometer to use. Apparently, the originator of this clever method had not pursued it far enought to discover it was not being done correctly.

THE TRUE FACTS

We all know that fish are cold-blooded, and that this means their body temperatures are regulated by the temperature of their immediate environment. If the water rises four degrees, so will the fish's temperature, and so on. But that isn't to say the two are identical. The fact is that most freshwater fish have a body temperature approximately one degree higher than the water they are in. This is due to the extra heat generated by normal bodily functions. Another fact: At least one degree is added during a typical angler-bass struggle. Fighting for your life, you'd put on a few degrees, too. So, when you take a bass's body temperature, subtracting two degrees from what the thermometer says should tell you almost exactly the temperature of the water from which he came. And that in turn can reveal his depth, among other vital pieces of information. We'll see how in just a minute.

THE PROPER THERMOMETER

There's really only one way to take a bass' temperature and that's with a *photographic thermometer*. It's the type photographers use to monitor the temperature of their chemicals in printing and developing. To list the attributes in order of importance:

- they are completely accurate (most electronic fishing thermometers are not.)
- they are consistently accurate, since they don't depend on batteries, which always run down.
- the reading is instantaneous.
- the sensitive thermister in the tip is able to touch the fish's stomach wall or contents, and thereby give a true reading of his temperature. (Most electronic thermometers, such as the one I was using that first time, protect their thermisters with strong metal ribs, which inhibit contact with the stomach and give off false readings.)
- their slender shafts and rounded tips slip effortlessly down a bass' throat — or up his other entrance, if you prefer.

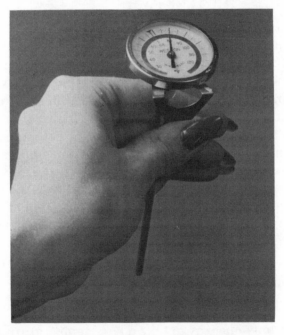

Photographic Thermometer

Since the photographic thermometer is so accurate, it can be used to check the accuracy of your other fishing thermometers. Most fishermen have a tendency to pull a new electronic thermometer out of the box, slap in a couple double-A's and start taking water temperatures, even though the directions say to first check the instrument's accuracy. Besides, to make this technique work, both your photographic thermometer and electronic thermometer must be synchronized, since one will be taking the bass' temperature and the other the water's.

Photographic thermometers are so compact you can carry one in your pocket for pond or river fishing. Yet they are durable enough to take all the abuse you can muster — believe me. They cost around $15 and can be found in most camera stores offering darkroom supplies. There are a number of brands available and I have found that some should be avoided. Before buying one, test it right there in the store. The thing to look for is a smooth unhesitating swing of the needle. Jerky types tend to stick on their way to the proper reading. The brand I recommend is Weston.

HOW BODY TEMPERATURES TELL DEPTH

Of course, this method is at its best during summertime, when a body of water has a change of temperature at almost every depth. Catch a bass, slip the photographic thermometer down his throat, subtract two degrees from the reading, then lower the electronic thermometer's probe over the side until it registers that same temperature. Chances are you'll be able to pinpoint the bass' depth to within a foot or two.

Unfortunately, it's not so cut-and-dried at other times of the year when the water is less stratified. But that doesn't mean this tactic cannot be just as deadly. To cite just one of many examples, a few Aprils ago, Larry Kauffman and I decided to entertain a few Lake Wapello largemouths. We arrived on the murky lake under a bright sky and promising southern breeze.

The surface temperature was 53 degrees. From one foot to seven feet it held a steady 52, then dropped to 50 for the remaining depths. Thinking the lunkers would probably be hanging around the seven-foot level, we both tied on medium-running Rebel-R's and concentrated on the rocky shores of the lake's north side. It took the better part of an hour, but Larry

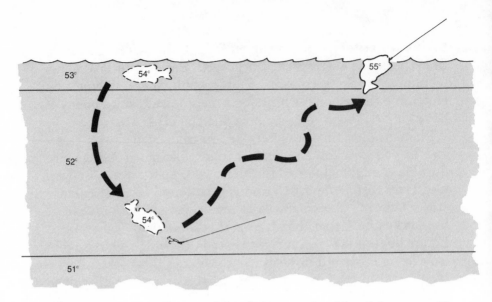

Figure 22. It's not all cut and dried. A struggle with a fisherman will raise a bass' body temperature one or two degrees; and the fish may have gone up or down for the lure, thereby showing his body temperature different from the water where he was apparently taken.

finally hauled in the first bass, a perky one-pounder. Once inserted, the photographic thermometer recorded 55 degrees. Subtracting two degrees (one for body heat, one for the struggle) gave us 53 degrees, the same as the lake's surface. Apparently, this particular bass had been hanging just under the surface. And since our Rebel-R's ran at about seven feet, that bass had gone *down* after the lure.

Needing no more proof, Larry switched to a shallow-running Rebel, while I decided to reserve judgment. Five minutes later he had two more nice bass in the boat.

"You just gonna sit there and watch me catch fish?" he asked. I admitted it was difficult, but that I felt there was still a chance the bigger bass were around seven feet. So I continued working deeper, telling myself this was the price a true researcher must sometimes pay.

Fifteen minutes and three non-keepers for Larry later, our first lunker zapped my *medium*-running Rebel. The bass aboard and the thermometer in place, what I fully expected to be a reading of a least one degree less than the others turned out to be one degree more—56! Subtracting the usual one degree for body heat, plus, this time, *two* degrees for the struggle, because it took longer, I came up with 53 degrees, just like before. As the very first bass had done, this one went down after the lure from his one-foot-deep holding area. I immediately tied on a shallow-runner crankbait and we both enjoyed fat-and-fast action for the next hour.

Without the photographic thermometer Larry Kauffman and I would undoubtedly have fished the seven-foot level all day, and just occasionally picked up bass hungry enough to dive for dinner. Consequently our "good" day would have been only "fair" and worst of all, we may never have known about all those bass that would have hit had the lure been coming right by their noses. It's very easy (and common) for an angler to believe a freshly taken bass came from the exact depth his lure was running, when in truth he may have come up or gone down after it. Taking body temperatures is about the only way to find out for certain. And when you consider that the closer a lure is to a bass, the more likely he is to hit it, it's well worth doing.

FORETELLING FEEDING SPELLS

It takes roughly 20 minutes for a fish's body temperature to completely adjust to a warmer or colder water temperature. In the first three minutes there is little change because it takes time for the new temperature to penetrate the muscle. From then on the stomach temperature changes rapidly and by the tenth minute the transition is almost completed.

Knowing about this "time to adjust" factor can occasionally let you know when a feeding spell is just starting. For example, one August day I was having a horrible time with the largemouths and was about to head in when I noticed a bass working the shallows. He attacked my first offering. Bringing his two-pound frame aboard, I was surprised to find a body temperature of 75 degrees — which meant he had to come from 73-degree water. The oddity was that the shallows he had come from were *80* degrees. It had to mean the fish had just moved up from cooler, deeper water, and was not the straggler I'd figured him for.

Although supper was waiting, I felt this may be the start of a major feeding period. So I continued working the shoreline, and saw more action in 15 minutes than I had seen all day. I owe that stringer — plus many others — to the photographic thermometer.

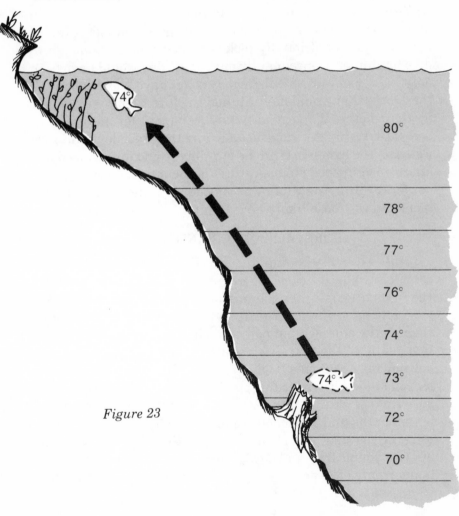

Figure 23

CONFIRMING IDEAL TEMPERATURES

Taking body temperatures can also give you an excellent indication of that one, best water temperature the bass in your lake prefer during summer stratification. I record on paper almost every bass temperature I take throughout the year, and by doing so have found a clear pattern to their thermal preferences. In early summer, for example, I've found that my bass' most common deep-water resting temperature is 72 degrees. By mid-summer it usually rises to around 74, due to the decreasing oxygen in the cooler depths. By late summer they are rarely found in water less than 76 degrees.

This can save you a lot of time by telling where to begin the search. Once the first bass is taken, the photographic thermometer then reveals whether he had just moved up, had been up for sometime, or was hanging down in the sanctuary.

A FINAL REMARK

Over the years I've run into a little skepticism concerning the value of taking fish's body temperatures, but in every case it came from someone who did not understand the system and certainly had never tried it. As you look down at that dial sticking out of a bass' mouth, staring back at you is a rather rare commodity in this mystical sport — a hard, solid fact! And it's something you can believe in. It may correct your mistakes and lead you to the bass or it may simply confirm that you were on the right track. Either way, it brings on a sense of confidence you'll never find by guessing.

Chapter 7
Finding the Best Depth

There is no need to expound on the importance of finding the depth of your bass during each outing. It's been the primary objective of fishermen since George Washington got skunked crossing the Delaware. Once you've located the bass vertically, the search is at least three-quarters over.

As you are about to see, this is often an easily accomplished feat. In fact, if you have read the chapters in Part One, you already have the knowledge and need only to piece the major variables into a complete picture. With a little practice and the proper equipment you will be able to calculate the bass' best depth(s) in about two minutes, provided you are familiar with the area's structure. It won't be correct every time, and rarely will you find all the bass at just that depth. But when compared to the time-consuming, trial and error approach used by most bass anglers today, you will be hours ahead. And that's not an exaggeration.

The best way to learn this system is to go over actual fishing

82

situations together. In each the secret is to uncover as much as possible about the following variables:

- structure
- water temperature
- angling pressure
- oxygen
- light penetration (water clarity)
- time of year and day
- climate (location of lake)
- weather

In any given situation most of these will *not* be factors, or at least not important ones. But over the course of a year, each will play its part in many of our lakes and ponds.

SITUATION 1

Time: Early March, 2 p.m.

Location: An impoundment in southern Arkansas.

Weather: The second day of a sunny, warming trend.

Structure: Having never fished this lake before, you select a likely-looking cove and scout the area thoroughly with your depth-finder. You find a creek channel, a small stumpy area in 15 feet of water, no weeds and a fair number of fallen shoreline trees.

Water temperature: By anchoring over the deepest part of the cove and taking a temperature reading at every depth, you find 51-52 degrees to be the lake's basic temperature, running from five feet down to the bottom at 25 feet. The brilliant sun, however, has warmed the upper extremeties to where the surface reads 57 degrees and three feet 55.

Oxygen: It's not worth taking a reading, since water this cold invariably has all the oxygen a fish could use at any depth in any state of activity.

Angling Pressure: Probably not a factor at this time of year, as most fishermen are home, believing it's too cold for fish to bite.

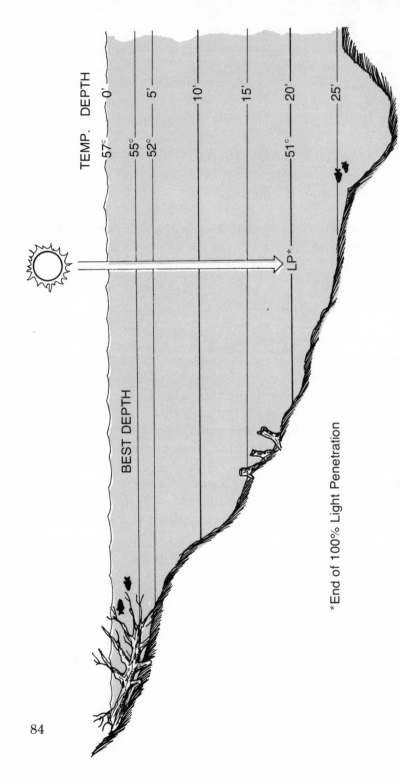

84

TEMP. DEPTH

57° 0'
55°
52° 5'
       10'
       15'
51° 20'
       25'

LP*

BEST DEPTH

*End of 100% Light Penetration

Figure 24. Situation 1. Structure and water temperature are really the only keys to the puzzle here. Between the surface and three feet represents the best conditions for feeding bass in the lake.

Light Penetration: The needle on your light meter drops below 100 percent when the probe hits 20 feet.

CONCLUSION:

Best Depth: 0 to 3 Feet. In this particular situation there are really only two pieces to the puzzle — structure and water temperature. That warm layer from the surface to three feet represents the best water conditions in the entire lake, so at least a few lunkers should be drawn to it. How many do come up and how long they stay depends on the quantity and quality of cover they find. If there were no shallow cover, such as those fallen trees, you'd probably be hard pressed to find any bass at 0-3 feet in this area and would be wise to try another cove.

For certain, bass will be found at other depths. But since a shallow bass is a feeding bass, you stand a much better chance working those shallow trees. If they fail to produce or if you are a devoted deep-water angler, you may want to try that channel dropoff. Down here, water temperature no longer counts because it is uniform. That leaves structure and to a lesser degree light penetration. Since sunlight is falling pretty heavily on those stumps, some bass may prefer the slightly darker water near the channel. This makes 25 feet the best resting depth in this immediate area, with 15 feet (at the stumps) a close second.

SITUATION 2

Time: Mid-June, 10 a.m.
Location: Northern Kentucky, five-year-old lake.
Weather: Not a factor here. It may be in how well the bass bite, but not in their depth.
Structure: You locate a cove that seems to have brushpiles at almost every depth.
Water Temperature: The lake is well stratified, beginning with 75 degrees at the surface. (See Figure 25.)

Oxygen: You can assume it's still too early in the summer for oxygen to be a problem or factor in the bass' depth, so no reading is necessary.

Angling Pressure: This being the favorite time of year for all fishermen, you find the lake somewhat "crowded."

Light Penetration: 100 percent light ends at 15 feet.

CONCLUSION

Best Depths: 3 to 5 Feet. This one is easy to figure, because there is really only one variable regulating the bass' depth. It's not structure, since there are numerous brushpiles and stumps at most depths. Nor is it light penetration, which rarely influences depth selection when good cover or stratified water is present. And of course it's not oxygen. That leaves water temperature.

Taking into account the time of year (mid-June) and this lake's lattitude (northern Kentucky) we can assume that 72 degrees is the bass' most ideal temperature. And 72 presently resides at the five-foot level. It may be tempting to believe that for resting purposes the bass will move down to enjoy the security of deep water, but all the security they need can be found by tucking into or under any one of the brushpiles or stumps in their ideal temperature. Going deeper would gain them only a colder, less desirable temperature. Granted, some may be found down deeper, but most will be up.

Actually, in this situation there is little difference between their best feeding and resting depths. It's here in the 3-5-foot layer that the bass find the best combination of temperature, structure and food. The 68 to 75 degree range in the top seven feet, plus bright sunlight, means a high concentration of plankton, and that in turn will draw the foodfish.

The only things keeping the surface-to-two-foot layer from being ideal are the 75-degree water and possibly the disturbance factor from too many anglers pounding the shoreline. Even without these variables, bass—especially the bigger ones — as a rule seem to prefer keeping a couple feet of water

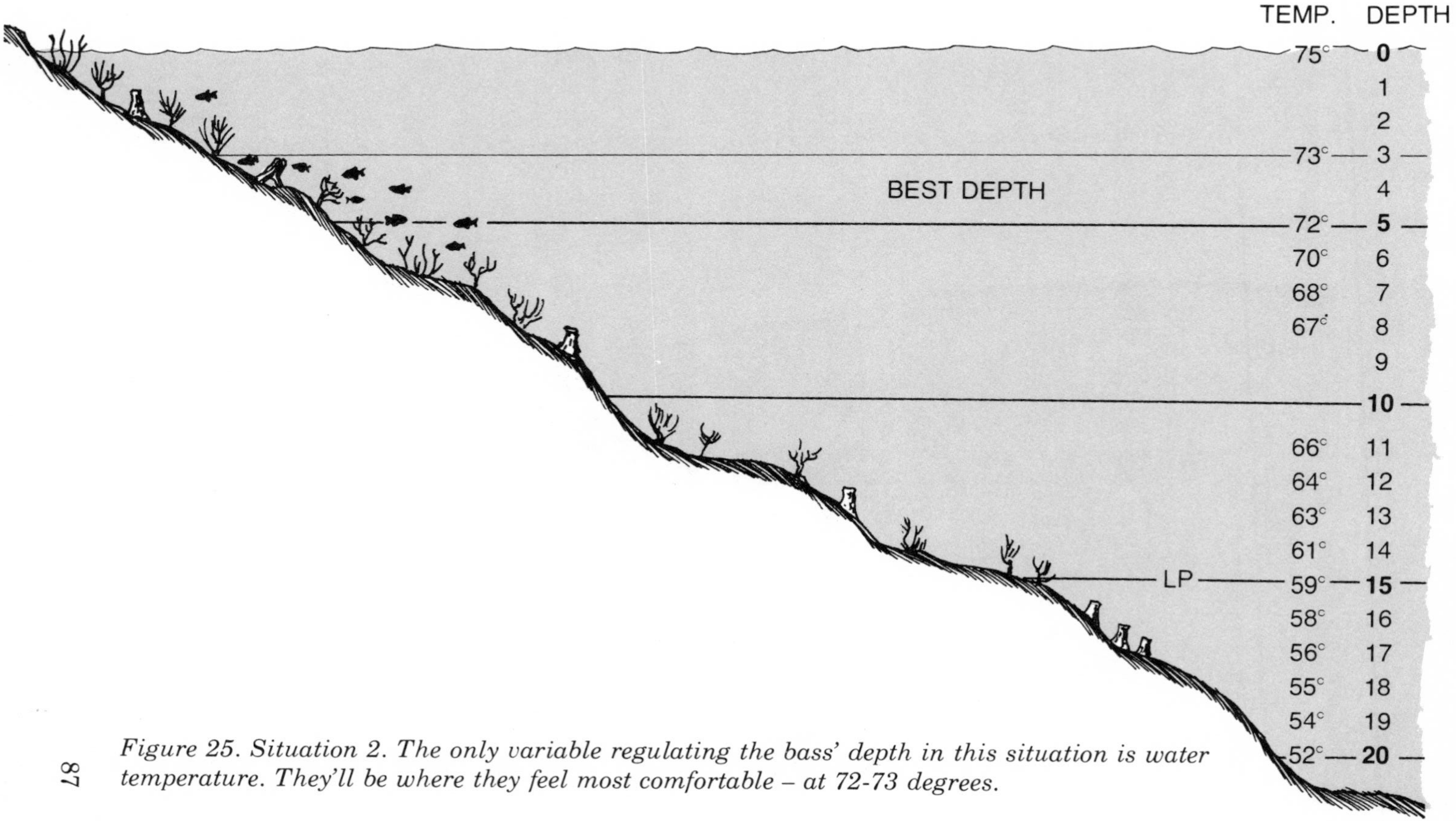

TEMP.	DEPTH
75°	0
	1
	2
73°	3
	4
72°	5
70°	6
68°	7
67°	8
	9
	10
66°	11
64°	12
63°	13
61°	14
59°	15
58°	16
56°	17
55°	18
54°	19
52°	20

BEST DEPTH

LP

Figure 25. Situation 2. The only variable regulating the bass' depth in this situation is water temperature. They'll be where they feel most comfortable – at 72-73 degrees.

87

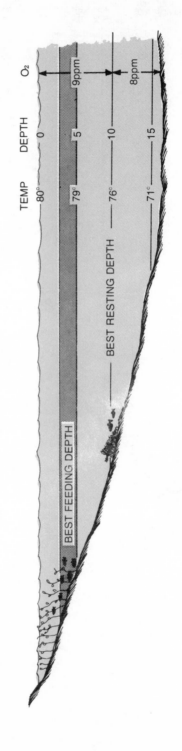

O₂   DEPTH   TEMP

←——— 9ppm ———→

←— 8ppm —→

0   80°

5   79°

BEST FEEDING DEPTH

10   76°

BEST RESTING DEPTH

15   71°

Figure 26. Situation 3. Common for farm ponds, structure plays the determining role in where the bass are.

between them and the surface, probably as a security cushion.

As a final note, this situation represents one of the few times of year when all the variables are favorable, or nearly so, to the bass. They can come shallow where all the food is, and stay as long as they like. Daily vertical migrations are not necessary. This is also the time you will find many bass in the latter stages of spawning.

SITUATION 3

Time: July 4, 9 a.m.
Location: A four-acre farm pond in Tennessee.
Weather: Not a factor
Structure: The pond is dishpanned, ringed with weeds down to five feet and your brother, who owns the land, says he sank a few Christmas trees at 10 feet in various places.
Water Temperature: 80 degrees on the surface and changing little down to ten feet. (See Figure 26.)
Oxygen: A steady 9 ppm down to 10 feet and 8 ppm thereafter.
Angling Pressure: Only your brother fishes the pond, and he hasn't for over a month.
Light Penetration: You meter still reads 100 percent light on the bottom at 15 feet.

CONCLUSION

Best Feeding Depth: 3 to 5 Feet. As is often true in farm ponds, here structure becomes the most determinant factor in the bass' depth. There are so few objects and irregularities that the bass will put up with slightly less than ideal temperatures in favor of relating to proper structure. A case in point is the weeds growing down to five feet. The temperature here is 79-80 degrees, not ideal, but still within their tolerance range for feeding. Virtually all the feeding will take place here, because this is where the food is. Crayfish and baitfish need cover as much as bass, and the weeds are about all they've got. If the water were to warm much more, the bass would still feed at the weeds, but probably in a series of shorter visits.

Best Resting Depth: 10 Feet. The same holds true while resting. Ideally, the bass would like to be at 12-13 feet in their ideal temperature of 73-74 degrees. (Remember, this is July in Tennessee.) But there is no structure present. So they move up to the Christmas trees, sacrificing a few degrees of comfort for an object to help them stay oriented. Take away the trees and you'd probably find the bass back down at 12-13 feet.

According to the Oxygen Table in Chapter Two, oxygen is not a factor in this situation, although it does come close and should be checked daily from here on. Light penetration, on the other hand, could be if you weren't careful. Obviously the water is quite clear, and it would be possible to spook a few shallow bass into deeper water by getting your body too close to the weeds. Remember, these bass have not been conditioned to much angling pressure.

SITUATION 4

Time: Late July, noon.
Location: A small impoundment in southern Illinois.
Weather: It's been hot and hazy for a week — "dog days."
Structure: Roughly half of the lake's perimeter has weeds which end at four feet. There is very little brush or similar structure, but the cove you decide to fish has a nice string of stumps and brushpiles down one side, plus a well-defined creek channnel.
Water Temperature: Of course, the lake is well stratified. The surface reads out at 86 degrees and the top of the "thermocline" — region of greatest temperature change — rests at about eight feet.
Oxygen: You find only 7 ppm just under the surface and the "oxycline" — last depth having sufficient oxygen for bass — at 10 feet.

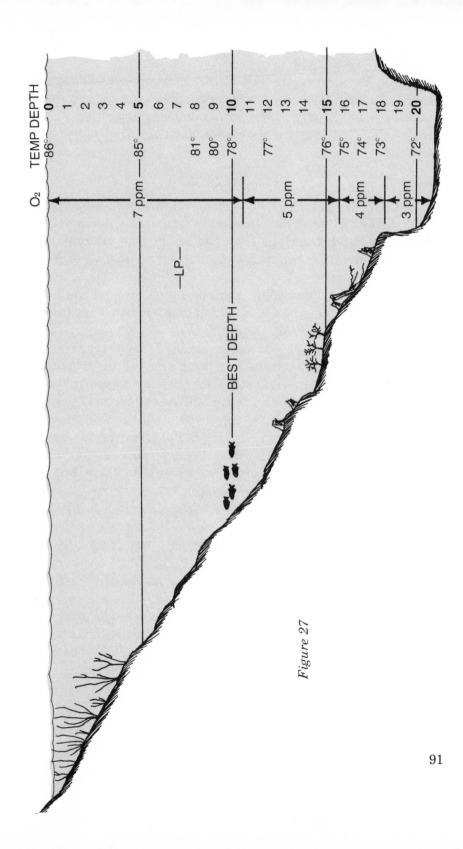

Figure 27

91

Angling Pressure: The "dog days" conditions may keep most bass fishermen home, but that contingent is more than made up for by the throngs of swimmers, boaters and skiers.

Light Penetration: 100 percent ends at seven feet.

CONCLUSION

Best Depth: Ten Feet. For so much of the year oxygen plays a small role, if one at all. Now comes late summer on a not-so-clear lake, and it springs from the wings like an applause-starved understudy, knocking most other variables out of the limelight.

The "time" and "location" variables suggest that the bass' ideal temperature is now about 75 degrees, which according to your readings, occurs at 16 feet. But as you can see, the fish cannot be here. The oxygen is too poor. (See the Oxygen Table in Chapter Two.) Nor can the bass hang next to any part of that brushline for the same reason. The bass are forced to swim shallower until they finally reach sufficient oxygen (7 ppm at 10 feet). And this is where they will stop, because moving shallower would gain them nothing but still warmer water. In essence, the bass are "sandwiched" between poor oxygen below and warm water above. It creates problems for them, but enables us to pinpoint their exact depth.

At the moment, you can expect little, if any, feeding. The bass certainly won't come up to do it. However, since these readings were taken at noon and the sun is out, by mid-to-late afternoon you may see a rise in oxygen content in the upper seven feet. (Plankton produce oxygen when struck by adequate sunlight, and your readings show that this light ends at seven feet.) The increase will be no more than a couple ppm and there's a slight chance it could be enough to bring a few bass to the weedline at four feet for a brief feed. Frankly, your best tactic would be to pack up and head for another lake with cleaner water or wait for a cold front to break up this horrendous set of circumstances.

When an oxygen problem hits a body of water, very few fishermen are aware of it. During the two-week period that I encountered the above situation, I neither saw nor heard of any other bass anglers who were working that 10-foot depth or, for that matter, even had an oxygen monitor. Most continued flogging the shorelines, while a few concentrated on the bass's ideal temperature down around 18-20 feet. My partners and I fished 10 feet exclusively. While our success ratio was barely "fair," it apparently was much higher than anyone else's.

A CLOSING NOTE

Please keep in mind that the term "best depth" does not necessarily mean the "only depth" at which you'll find bass. It is simply that one layer of water offering the most favorable combination of structure, water temperature, oxygen and other variables, thereby making it the most logical place to find most of the bass.

Also, once you have calculated what seems to be a well-defined "best depth", such as during summer stratification, don't abandon it if a bass isn't taken right away. While you probably have found them vertically, the crosshairs are not complete until you've located their horizontal placement as well. (Which is rather easy, since bass are notorious for congregating around points, timberlines, creek channels, etc.) If, on the other hand you feel you are zeroed in, then by all means be patient. Despite what we want to believe, bass spend far more time tight-lipped than in a positive feeding mood, so you may have to wait them out. Without question, one of the most common and disastrous pitfalls of this sport is mistaking turned-off bass for bass that aren't there.

Chapter 8
Avoiding Costly Mistakes

Big bass are wary. In fact, that's partly the reason they became big bass. Without a deep-seated fear of his enemies, a largemouth today is lucky if his third birthday isn't celebrated in beer-batter. Consequently, the angler with trophy on his mind should put as much caution into his game plan as the lunker has in his.

Common sense tells us not to roar the outboard right up to where we plan to cast, or drop a tackle box on the floor of an uncarpeted boat. It also says to keep our distance while casting so the fish won't be frightened by our image. But that's where some trophy hunters go wrong. In fact, based on what science tells us about a fish's ability to see above the surface, it's possible that for every lunker caught, at least two others, just as catchable, are spooked before the lure even hits the water.

Figure 28 gives us a rough idea of how close we can get to a bass without its seeing us under ideal visibility conditions. It is drawn to scale for a six-foot angler going after a lunker in five feet of water. Note that while standing on a raised deck, such as that found on a high-performance bassboat, he should stay approximately 33 feet away to keep from being seen. Were he to sit, he could move in five feet closer. And, if sitting in a more typical fishing boat, the angler could edge in yet another five

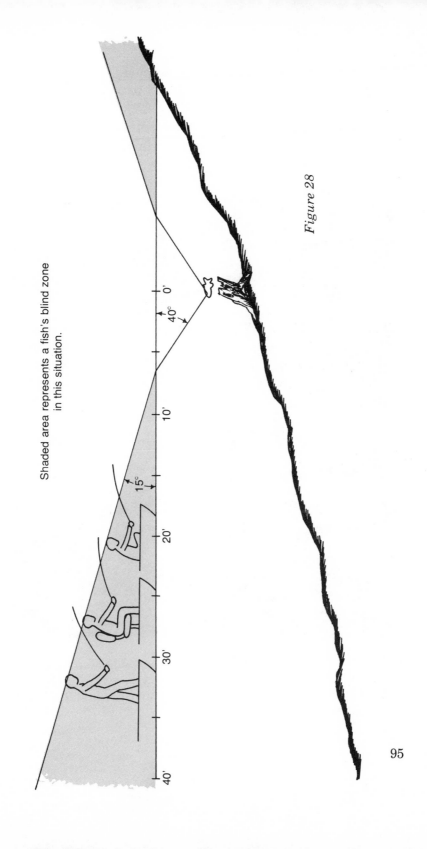

Shaded area represents a fish's blind zone in this situation.

Figure 28

feet. Also, since it is generally recommended that you cast a lure beyond where the fish is believed to be, another ten feet should be added to these distances.

What Frightens Bass. Now to the finer points. At ranges of 15 feet and more, it's not your image alone that spooks the fish — it's any *sudden movement,* such as a casting motion. As a

Preferring to stand while fishing, even under high-visibility conditions, this angler avoids spooking bass by staying well back from his target (the emerged stump) and casting 10-15 feet beyond it.

result, developing a sidearm cast can be most beneficial. It keeps virtually all your movement closer to the water and therefore more out of the fish's line of vision, allowing you to move in closer to the target.

For example, in a clear-water rock quarry I fish, there's a rockpile ten feet from shore that frequently harbors bass I can see. If I approach it on foot slowly and quietly, waving my rod as if to cast overhand, they'll scatter when I'm approximately 35 feet away. If, instead, I fake sidearm casts, the bass won't spook until I'm inside the 25-foot marker. And with no casting motion whatsoever, I can get within 15 feet. So, if you must cast overhand, you'd better stick to the distances shown in Figure 28.

How Far Can You Cast Accurately. The problem, of course, is that the farther you stay back from your target, the more difficult it is to make an accurate cast. Tests show that the effective casting range of the average angler is a maximum of 30 feet. For the highly skilled, it's up to 40 feet. True, you can throw much farther — 60 feet or more — but with considerably less accuracy. Once you've determined your ideal range (the back yard and a measuring tape is the best method) the diagram will show what position(s) you can assume without frightening the bass. If it's 30 feet, for example, perhaps you'd be better off by staying seated in most shallow-water, high-visibility situations.

When Bass Become Less Wary. So far, we have been talking only about those times when the bass' ability to see us and his state of caution are maximal. There are instances when you can move in much closer without frightening even the most prudent old-timer. The most obvious is when he is in *deep water* — more than five feet in murky water, more than 10-15 feet in clear. Not only does the extra water between his world and ours make a bass feel more secure, it clouds and disperses the fisherman's image, making him appear less threatening. So, if you are a staunch deep-water angler, you may as well stick these past few pages on the bottom of the bird cage.

Other times include: *murky water; when the surface is broken by heavy wave action; and when fishing at night.* In all instances the bass' vision into our world is greatly restricted, lulling him into a sense of security. The same is true when the bass is tucked into dense cover or against a structure that at least partially blocks his upward view, such as lily pads, thick weeds or standing trees.

The hungrier a bass is, the dumber he seems to be. I'm sure many of you have been on the water when the bass were committing gang suicide over your lure. Whatever causes this marvelous phenomenon, your presence seems to matter little to the fish. In a sense, the same thing happens continuously in *waters overpopulated with bass.* Competition among them can be so strong that even the lunkers must forego security in favor of spearing a meal. And, finally, is the case of the *spawning bass.* Ruled almost entirely by instinct to protect the nest, a bedding bass is rarely frightened off by the sight of an angler. It can, however, cause him to ignore your lure, even if it falls perfectly into the nest. It would be better if you marked the spot, came back later and cast from a distance beyond the bass' line of vision.

Tips When Visibility Is High. Whenever possible, cast away from the sun. True, your shadow may fall on the water, but that's better than your image, lighted up in all its splendor. It also forces the bass to look into the sun to see you — an old Indian trick from the John Wayne late movies. Wear dark, unassuming clothing, and avoid bright colors and shiny surfaces on your lures, rods and boat. Finally, if possible, go alone. Comradeship is one of the best aspects of fishing, but when it comes to gumshoeing Old Maude, one angler is four times better than two.

GETTING THE LURE TO THE BASS

In April a few years ago, my local bass club held a tournament on Lake Stockton, Missouri for the first time. As is so often the case, we ran head-on into a vicious cold front, sporting a temperature of 50 degrees, a relentless 30 mph west wind and periodic thunderstorms. But the shoreline cover was everywhere and excellent in the form of weeds, buckbrush, stumps and fallen trees. Most of us agreed that under these conditions the bass would be tucked tightly into this cover.

It didn't take long to discover, however, that in most areas, the wood and weeds were so thick we simply could not cast effectively into it. So, rather than going after the bulk of the bass and certainly losing many lures, we worked the outside edges, hoping at least a few mavericks would be out and feeding. Some were, but most were only in the 10-12-inch class.

Two weeks later I was talking with Jim Rogers, a tournament professional and resident of the Stockton area. I was to learn that he had been fishing the lake the same day and had done quite well — ten times better than our best stringer, to be exact. I silently credited his success to knowing the hotspots, until upon further questioning I discovered that he had been working the same shallow cover as we had. The only difference, it turned out, was that while we fished along the outside edges, trying to coax the bass out, Jim was right in the thick of things, taking his lure to them.

Jim Rogers knew that conventional methods would be futile under those circumstances, so he broke out his seven-foot "Flippin'" rod with 25-pound test monofilament and a half-ounce jig-n-eel. With his boat sitting where we were casting, he flipped the lure well back into the jungle, not minding at all if the line draped over a twig or floating log. He then jigged the offering up and down in the same place about 20 times or until a bass struck. About 40 did.

There are two parts to this lesson. First, *never give up on a sure-fire bass area until you've tried everything to get at them.* And certainly don't forego that area because you are bent on using a favorite lure and don't want to lose it. The second part falls right in line with the first — *always select a lure (or technique) first by its ability to work the area you most want to fish.*

For example, say you feel certain the best place for big bass is the pockets in the middle of a broad, thick weedbed. But every cast with your reliable crankbait, spinnerbait or plastic worm comes back with five pounds of slime. Don't switch targets, switch lures or techniques. Try a weedless spoon or a plastic worm with no weight, even if you have no confidence in either. Run to the nearest sporting goods store and buy a 16-foot cane pole so you can drop a jig or spinner straight down into the pockets. Do whatever it takes to effectively work that area you most believe in. Only then should you worry about color, size, presentation, etc.

FACT OR FAIRY DUST

There is much to be gained from fishing or palavering with other bass anglers, from joining a bass club, participating in or observing a tournament and reading the various outdoor publications. So, by all means be inquisitive. Be a student. And most of all, be a listener. In fact, show me a person who would rather listen than talk when the subject is bass, and I'll show you someone who is either a crackerjack angler or very soon will be. Who was it that said, "When you're talking, everything's going out and nothing's coming in."

Unfortunately, there can sometimes be a problem with tapping these outside sources: You can't always be certain of their credibility. While the vast majority of fellow fishermen will shoot you the truth, even the most honest man may unintentionally mislead you if he misinterpreted the facts or excluded a vital ingredient. Then there are those overzealous few who just can't bake anything without adding a little spice. And, of course, the secretive soul who doesn't have the heart to say, "I'd rather not tell you," so he spins a straight-faced fabrication that will protect both his "secret" and his reputation as a nice guy. Anytime knowledge comes second-hand, you are at the mercy of someone else's judgment.

Over the years, my researching of this sport has depended on a wide variety of sources, so I've had to assess which people and things are the most reliable and to what degree. Below, listed in order, are those you are most likely to encounter, plus a brief explanation of why I have so rated each. For you seasoned bass fishermen my lists will just confirm what you probably already know.

CREDIBILITY LIST

Scientific Facts. These are usually the most dependable, being the result of highly-trained, well-equipped scientists, working in carefully controlled conditions with one common goal — to uncover the truth.

Your Own Experience. This is the only place from which to gain information first-hand. But before drawing any firm conclusions, you would be wise to confirm them with a few other reliable sources.

The Experience of a Trusted Friend. Just one good friend can double your information intake. But since most of it will come second-hand, ask a lot of questions and take nothing as gospel.

Books, Articles, Lectures, etc. People in this line usually have careers at stake. So if their teachings do not help you catch bass, they may be out of work. In some cases you have to use your judgment, because they may be referring to waters, styles or goals different from your own.

Most Marina and Resort Owners. Once you are their customer, these folks can be good to talk to just before heading out to fish. Most keep up on things so you'll catch bass and come back again.

BLACKLIST

A Tournament Contestant Before the Event Is Over. He isn't about to give anything away, so you shouldn't even ask. Afterwards he may tell some truth, especially if his partners are standing there to keep him honest.

The Two Winners of a Buddy Tournament. There will probably be another tourney on the same waters with these guys as partners again, so revealing their winning pattern would be foolish.

The Story-Teller. This one can be tough to finger, because he is very convincing. He rarely gets skunked and usually loses a real whopper every time out. Those big ones he does catch are released or eaten immediately without being recorded on film or witnessed. Most of the time he fishes alone or with someone you never heard of. When he does go out with a mutual acquaintance, he has one of his few bad days. Enjoy his stories, but nothing more.

Market Information. Data gained via salesmen, advertising or booklets published by manufacturers may be basically factual, but it is probably very one-sided. After all, their business is not catching bass, it's catching you. *Caveat emptor.*

Perhaps the best general advice is to be skeptical — but not incredulous — of everyone and everything until you've had a fair chance to prove or disprove the information for yourself. In most cases the fastest way to do that is by having a sound, factual foundation of bass knowledge already in your head. As the data comes in, you can analyze it for feasibility, judge it for importance, then file it into its proper place right on the spot.

LOCATING RESTING BASS IN SUMMER

It's late summer as you launch your boat on a not-so-clear lake you've never fished before. To learn as much as quickly as

WHICH DEPTHS TO SEARCH FOR BASS-HOLDING STRUCTURES

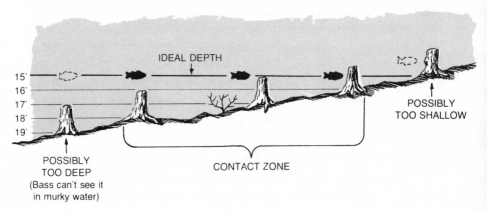

15'
16'
17'
18'
19'

IDEAL DEPTH

POSSIBLY
TOO SHALLOW

POSSIBLY
TOO DEEP
(Bass can't see it
in murky water)

CONTACT ZONE

possible, you take oxygen and temperature readings and discover that the bass are probably sandwiched into a very narrow band of water (we'll say 15 feet). Now, since all that's left to do is find the structures holding them at that depth, you begin motoring along the 15-foot contour with your eye glued to the depth-finder. Right?

Wrong! Have a look at Figure 29.

As you can see, by scouting along the 15-foot contour you'd undoubtedly miss the bass. Rarely will largemouths — particularly resting ones — be smack on the bottom. They almost always suspend. Also, their ability to see objects under water depends heavily on the water's clarity, which in this case means only a few feet, at best. So you should move out to where the bottom reads at least 16 feet and look for those structures which rise up to or near that ideal 15-foot layer.

EMOTION VERSUS RESULTS

The final tip is that you give the other four a chance. I realize one or more may go a little against your grain as each did mine. But once you have tested them for yourself, I'm certain you will be convinced of their worth. For example, spend a month, season or even a year keeping a low profile in lunker waters, then compare the results with an equal period of time when you didn't. This may sound bold, but with all other conditions being equal, I guarantee your lunker score will be higher. The first year I tried it, my take of big bass more than doubled that of the previous year. Only then was I a believer in what science had been saying all along.

So, allow your intellect free reign now and then. Sure, you want to believe casting your favorite lure into open water will bring in as many bass as yo-yoing an ugly jig beneath yonder maze of logs, or that everything people tell you is true, or that bass always lie smack on the bottom. But what you want to believe can easily get in the way of what you really want. And in this instance, I presume that's more and bigger bass.

103

Chapter 9
Lunker Days

Any knowledgeable bassman will tell you that certain days are better than others for taking big bass. In fact, the larger the fish, the fewer good days there are. Knowing ahead of time when these lunker days will occur may not be that important to the man who fishes every day, but to the other 99 percent who must divide their time between fishing and the forty thousand duties of husbandry and fatherhood, it can mean everything. Hours on the lake are precious and few, and in the case of lunker hunting they must be chosen wisely.

Fortunately, there are definite patterns to the types of days big bass hit best. I began uncovering these patterns in 1971 by keeping very detailed, daily fishing logs. The procedure I used was to take the date every lunker bass was caught by myself, friends and anyone else who would confide in me, plus all those on record with the state conservation commission, bass clubs and sporting goods stores, then compare them with changes in weather (sun, wind, air temperature, etc.) and water conditions (temperature, oxygen, light, etc.). Certain unmistakable patterns emerged, and I have since confirmed them every year.

HOW TO SELECT SPRING "LUNKER DAYS"

Following are listed what I have found to be eight of the most important points in picking that right day in the spring. Please keep in mind these pertain only to *lunker* bass — fish which have been around for at least five years. Compared to their smaller brethren, big bass are far more cautious, clever and set in their ways. They hunt mostly from ambush, and while the younger ones feed almost continuously, the big ones are opportunists.

1—The primary prerequisite for a spring lunker day (and I cannot stress this enough) is that the water, particularly in the first five feet, must be *warming*. At the very least, it must be holding after a period of warming. Being cold-blooded, a bass' state of activity depends vastly on the temperature of his surroundings. Warming water acts as a stimulus, firing up his metabolism and urging him to feed. Cooling water does the opposite. My records over the years show that only four percent of all lunkers taken were caught from cooling water. And then it was only on the first cold day after a considerable warming trend, before the water had cooled more than two degrees.

2—A day with a sharp rise in water temperature is better than one with a gradual rise. The faster the warming the greater the stimulus.

3—The *first* day of a *good* warming trend is usually better than the following days. This time it's because the stimulus is sudden. Due to the previously cooling water, the bass probably fed poorly, so an abrupt improvement of conditions may drive them to the shallows to make up for lost time. And since the previous days probably saw far less pressure from fishermen, the bass shouldn't be too spooky.

4—On the other hand, during a *gradual* warming trend (one-degree rise in water temperature per day) the second or third day is often better. Apparently one degree just doesn't have the spark to fire up a fish.

5—Sunny, windless days, even if cool, can be excellent, especially in the spring. With a calm surface, the sun can warm the shallows as much as ten degrees, creating a layer of heaven for bass, who are perpetually seeking their ideal temperature of 68 to 75 degrees. If your lake or pond has good shallow cover, you will normally find the bass there in the mid-afternoon, when the sun is warmest. If it doesn't, hit them a few hours later when the water is warmest and the sun's penetration has diminished somewhat.

6—Late in the spring when the water temperature is over 70, the *first cloudy day* after a few sunny ones can be one of the best times of all, particularly in clear water. Again, it's because of a *sudden* stimulus. The once-bright shallows are now dimly lighted, giving the bass some visual edge over their prey, beckoning them to stay in the feeding grounds all day. As a rule, the heavier the overcast the better.

7—We still don't know exactly why, but some of the best bassing comes just before a front moves in. The fish may turn on half a day before it arrives, but the best time seems to be just an hour or two before, or when the advance cloud bank first covers the sun. The worst fronts are usually the best.

8—Winds from the *southern* half of the compass are generally better, partly because of the warming trends associated with them and partly because of the wave action they generate on northern shores, which are warmer in the spring and therefore good bass attractors.

COLD WATER

Too many bassing hopefuls let cold water frighten them away in the early spring. My records show that a high percentage of a year's huge bass are taken from water colder than 50 degrees. I believe this is due mostly to "pecking orders," which means the toughest and biggest fish take the best spots. In the case of early to mid-spring, when the prey pickings are slim, you can bet it will be the sag-belly bass who own the lake's best ambushing cover during a "lunker day." The next largest bass will be in the next best cover, and so on down the line, culminating with the dinks, who must often settle for each other's company in deeper water.

Also, it's the lunkers who are the hungriest by winter's end, having fed less than the smaller bass during the past months. So they are more likely to be in a feeding mood now, even if the water is only 45 degrees. You may get only one hit in four hours at this time of year, but the odds are good it will be a bass of considerable size.

The "pecking order" phenomenon slowly tapers off, then ends when the spawning urge takes over as the shallows approach 60 degrees. Until then, there may be times when it becomes disrupted, such as on days when the fishing pressure is heavy. Too much above-surface activity can drive the big bass out of the shallows and into the security of deep water. An omen of this is when you start catching one-pounders off prime shallow structures during a lunker day.

HOW WEATHER AFFECTS WATER TEMPERATURE

As you have seen, the major key to a "lunker day" is warming water. So, to accurately predict a next day's lunker potential, you have to know whether the shallows will be rising or falling in temperature. Unless you live on a lake and can take the temperature three or four times a day, you'll need a basic understanding of weather's effect on water temperature.

Some days are fairly obvious, like when our well-endowed TV weather girl says tomorrow will be 70 degrees, and it's only mid-March. But others are more tricky, and you may not know if it's a day for trophy hunting or household duties. Often, the subtle lunker days are the best because with most fishermen thinking the weather's wrong, the lake will be quiet and the lunkers less spooky, not to mention the lack of competition.

Figure 30	BEST DAYS FOR SPRING LUNKERS (How Weather Affects Water Temperature			
Weather Conditions	Air Warmer Than Water	Lunker Potential	Air Cooler Than Water	Lunker Potential
Sunny, Calm	Extreme shallows may warm 5-10°	Good	Extreme shallows may warm 4-8°	Good
Sunny, Breezy	One to five feet may warm 4-5°	Good	One to five feet may warm 4-8°	Fair to Good
Sunny, Windy	Entire lake may warm 3-4°	Good	Entire lake may cool slightly	Poor to Fair
Cloudy, Calm	Little change	Excellent*	Little change	Excellent*
Cloudy, Breezy	Entire lake may warm 2-3°	Good to Excellent	Entire lake may cool 1-2°	Poor
Cloudy, Windy	Entire lake may warm 2-4°	Good to Excellent	Entire lake may cool 2-4°	Poor
*Lunker potential is "excellent" if following warming or stable period; otherwise, "fair to good."				

Figure 30 gives a general illustration of the effects of sun, wind, and air temperature on water. The chart can serve as an excellent guide in determining lunker days in the spring. For example, say tomorrow is supposed to be sunny, windy and have a high of 52 degrees. What's the decision? Do you go fishing tomorrow or get the cat spayed?

Under "weather conditions" on the left side of the chart you locate "sunny and windy," then slide over to the "air cooler than water" column on the right side. You'll find that the entire lake may cool somewhat, and consequently the lunker potential is only "Poor-to-Fair." In this instance, the culprit is the wind mixing the cool air into the warmer water, causing the water temperature to drop. And there is no real help from the sun's warming rays, because they are blocked and scattered by the wave action.

But had there been no wind that day, the water would have lost little if any heat to the air and the sun would have penetrated nicely, warming the shallows noticeably. That would have made it a "lunker day" — probably one that most fishermen would ignore. I did once a few years ago, and one of my friends caught the lake's largest bass in many years. This same effect, of course, can occur even on windy days if your lake has sheltered coves.

SUMMER LUNKER DAYS

Once the bass have finished spawning and are settled into a summer routine, it's much more difficult to forecast upcoming lunker days. In the spring, the weather was our guide, but since it now has stabilized pretty much, there are few sudden stimuli to send most lunkers on simultaneous feeding sprees. Actually, the angler should concentrate more on hitting the right time of day — which is the subject of the next chapter.

Still, there is one particular weather condition that definitely merits mention. Many times I've seen it spontaneously turn the bass into ravenous feeders. Usually they were of all sizes, but once it seemed to affect only the big fellows. And my partner and I always had them to ourselves, which isn't too surprising when you consider that in every case the "big turn-on" was sparked by the passing of a *severe cold front!*

Actually, the effects of fronts on bass fishing depend on the time of year. In the spring and fall they can be disastrous, mainly because the temperature of an entire lake usually drops at least a few degrees after its passing, creating a negative stimulus on the fish. But during the summer, most of a lake is protected by the warm, upper layers, which absorb the brunt of the front's effects and render the "damage" minimal.

Then there's the one special time of late summer. Here, a properly timed severe cold front can be tremendous. By late July many bass waters are locked into "dog days" — that poor fishing period characterized by hot water, low oxygen, a dwindling food supply and a prolonged phase of muggy, unchanging weather. A *mild* front here would probably do little, but a severe one can really fire up the bass. By cooling the water quickly back to a more comfortable range, it improves the oxygen supply. (The cooler the water, the more oxygen it can hold.) This, coupled with the fact that the bass probably haven't eaten much lately, literally drives them to the shallows in bunches.

For example, right after such a late-summer cold front in 1976 I took 19 keeper smallmouths from the base of a stump in under an hour — 14 on consecutive casts. Meanwhile, my partner, John Newton, did virtually the same thing not more than 100 yards away. Then in early September of 1977 I pulled in over 40 pounds of largemouths ranging from one to five pounds in two hours from a small Iowa lake that had produced poorly all year. One old catfisherman on the shore probably thought I was a demigod of the angling arts, but my skills were simply in knowing what to look for in the weather. The bass did the rest.

PREDICTING THIS TURN-ON

Exactly when it occurs in your area depends on the climate and preceding weather. In my region of southeastern Iowa, it normally hits sometime between early August and early September, as the first Arctic cold front of the season rolls through,

110

Figure 31

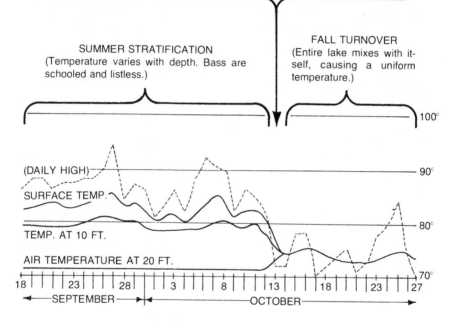

LOOK FOR FEEDING FRENZY
(The main clue is a super cold front with strong winds coming at the end of summer's warm weather. The sudden drop in air temperature cools the lake's upper layers, and the winds mix them with the lower layers, causing every depth to change in temperature. Notice that the lower depths actually *warm up*. This drastic transition acts as a strong stimulus to bass.

SUMMER STRATIFICATION
(Temperature varies with depth. Bass are schooled and listless.)

FALL TURNOVER
(Entire lake mixes with itself, causing a uniform temperature.)

100°

(DAILY HIGH) — 90°

SURFACE TEMP.

TEMP. AT 10 FT. — 80°

AIR TEMPERATURE AT 20 FT.

70°

18   23   28   3   8   13   18   23   27
◄—SEPTEMBER—►◄————————OCTOBER————————►

reminding folks that fall is in the wings. This front causes one of the most drastic changes of the year in any body of water.

As shown in Figure 31, before the front's passing, the water is still stratified thermally from summer. Then, almost overnight, the cold air and strong winds cool the warm upper layers and they mix with the entire lake or pond. As a result *every* depth experiences a change in temperature. The top layers

111

cool, the lower depths warm, averaging out to a uniform and very desirable temperature of 70 to 74 degrees. The oxygen also improves. The water now is beginning what scientists call "fall turnover," and it is often the best news the bass have had in months.

This feeding frenzy does not always run in conjunction with "fall turnover" however. For instance, July of 1974 was the victim of a long heat wave, where surface temperatures boiled in the 90's and the oxygen content in most comfortable depths was inadequate. Bass fishing in my area meant sitting by the air conditioner, casting practice plugs at the latest issue of *Bassmaster Magazine*. Then, on August 1 a real "norther" howled out of Canada and chased the heat wave into the South where it belonged. The next day found the skies a crisp blue, the air a chilly 72 degrees and the wind moving out of the northwest. Incredibly, the water temperature was suddenly a uniform 78 degrees down to 20 feet, and my car and trailer were the only ones in the ramp parking lot. My regular bass fishing buddy and I didn't find a true feeding frenzy, but we landed more lunkers in that short afternoon than in any other day of the entire year, including my two largest bass of the year.

So, in a nutshell, this "summer lunker day" can — and probably will — happen anytime a passing cold front turns unfavorable water conditions into more suitable ones. Sometime within that first or second day following the front, the bass fishing could really get hot. In my experience, the feeding has always begun after noon, continued to twilight and lasted for that day only. I believe it could go on for at least another day in large lakes with good bass populations.

Bass are usually schooled and very competitive, so lure selection is wide open. The schooling also means you must keep moving until contact is made. For me, structures based in relatively deep water and rising near the surface — such as trees or large brushpiles or submerged creek channels — pay off better than just indiscriminately plugging the shorelines. But the most important thing to do is *stay confident*. That's no

small task, since going fishing after a cold front violates what is normally considered to be a fundamental law of good bass fishing.

FALL LUNKER DAYS

If you know how to predict spring "lunker days," you are in good shape for the fall. There are, however, a couple notable differences. First, if you wait for warming water, the lake may not see you again until next spring. Obviously, the trend in the fall is toward a steady decline in water temperature, with only intermittent and generally weak periods of warming. When a warm spell of weather does occur, key more on the latter part of it, as the first day probably did no more than halt the cooling of the water. Also, even though the sun hangs at a lower angle now, it is the water's major source of heat, so try to fish those calm sunny days.

The other difference is that you will rarely catch just lunkers on an ideal day. In fact, it's the smaller bass that seem more bent on feeding in the fall. Schooled more — and therefore aggressive — they apparently rebel against the laws of "pecking order" by inhabiting the good cover areas and attacking anything within range. Perhaps it's the lunkers' turn to settle for scraps. My advice would be to fish for bass en masse and take the lunkers as they come.

114

Chapter 10
Prime Times

While Chapter Nine dealt with the types of days bass could be expected to hit the best, this one zeroes in on the better times of any given day. It may surprise some of you to learn that these prognostications are not based on moon phases, computer computations or whether the cows in the meadow are up and feeding, interesting as each may be. Instead, like most other tips and techniques throughout this book, they are the result of scientific facts, applied logic and the accumulative experience of many expert bass fishermen. I trust you'll find these suggested "prime times" to be, in the long run, more helpful than any other you may have read before.

THE SPECIFICS OF PRIME TIMES

The older and larger a bass becomes, the less effective he is at running down prey in the open. So, "calculated" ambushing is his most widely used tactic. By "calculated" I mean that through years of conditioning the bass has learned how to put most of the odds in his favor to achieve a successful feeding. First, he knows that the shallower he comes, the more food he'll find. Secondly, his body tells him that it operates better in warm water than in cold — that is, up to his ideal temperature of 70 to 75 degrees. And thirdly, the lower the light level, the more visual edge he has over his prey.

Now, with these factors in mind, ask yourself this: "At what time of each day will the *shallows* come the closest to the bass' ideal 70-75 degrees and light level?" It's only logical that the one time of day offering the most favorable conditions would be a major consideration for feeding. I began asking myself that question in 1971, and the results proved highly successful. It was particularly gratifying, then, to poll many experts across the country and find the vast majority's prime times concurred with mine in most instances.

The best biting time of day to go for bass changes from season to season, creating basically four different periods over the course of a year. And in each transition the temperature of the water is the primary key. As we discuss each of the four, you will see how water temperature and sunlight interact to bring about each day's prime time.

EARLY SPRING PRIME TIME

From a water temperature standpoint this early spring period begins when the water warms a few degrees for the first time of the year and ends when the shallows eventually hit about 60 degrees. The prime time to nail a bass on a warm sunny day would be from around *noon to 4 p.m.* because the shallows are at their warmest of the day. Many fish, including items on the bass' menu, seek out this extra warmth. In the early stages of this period the upper layers may be only 48 degrees while the rest of the lake is 45 or less. Those few degrees of warmth can stimulate a fish's metabolism, thereby making him more active. Also, a fish's dark body is capable of soaking up more of the sun's heat than can most water, so they often "bask" just under the surface, resulting in a body temper-

116

ature a degree or two higher than the surrounding water. This fires his metabolism even further.

Unfortunately, with all this wonderful heat from the sun comes a lot of bright light — not one of the bass' favorite things. Exposing them to the smaller baitfish, it makes feeding more difficult. But this time of year, temperature is still the bass' largest concern, so the brightness must be tolerated. Actually, "compensated for" would be a better term, since the bass beat the light factor by simply hiding in or around good cover.

Determining the prime time on a *cloudy* day is another matter. If it occurs later on in this period, say in water in the mid-to-high 50's, and comes after a period of warm weather, the fishing is usually fair, but steady throughout most of the day. The warming water called the bass up and the sudden low light level invites them to stay and partake. On the other hand, cloudy days during periods of cooling generally have no prime time whatsoever. The bass are turned off and your best tactic may be to come back when the weather turns favorable once again.

About the time the water reaches 55 degrees, secondary prime times may develop around mid-morning on sunny days, then possibly again about 6 p.m. These are characterized by taking four or five bass in about an hour, then not being able to buy a strike for the next two. I've seen days where these two secondary spells, strung together with the prime time of mid-day, make it appear the bass are hitting all day non-stop. But by and large, concentrating your efforts between the hours of 10 a.m. and 4 p.m. — with special emphasis on noon to 2 p.m. — will bring the best results.

LATE SPRING PRIME TIME

As the three-to-five-foot level approaches and passes 60 degrees, the male bass begin sifting into the shallows to work their tails off preparing spawning nests. The females, meanwhile, also become more shallow bound, but still for the purpose of feeding. This casts the mold for more than one daily

117

prime time during the early part of this period.

The females and non-nesting males continue much as before, preferring the heat of the day for feeding, with perhaps a gradual expansion into the slightly earlier and later hours — 9 a.m. and 5 p.m. Obviously, this makes the prime time less distinct, but it does not distract from its quality. The good fishing period is simply lengthened. The sun is still the key, as evidenced by poorer fishing on cloudy days and by the way bass frequently turn on just minutes after an overcast afternoon turns to clear skies.

Then there's the nest-building males. Paternal instincts have them marching to a different drummer through most of the day, as they seem much more interested in preparing and protecting their own private plot of ground than in running down a meal. By 5 p.m., however, this all changes. Once the sun no longer falls heavily on the nest, the males are apparently free to serve their stomachs' needs. This prime time is easily missed by many anglers, because once a nesting male is taken, you won't catch another until you move to another nest. And if you're not working the spawning grounds, it may seem there's no feeding activity.

As late spring progresses and the water temperature starts closing in on the bass' ideal 68 to 75 degrees, a new and very distinctive prime time evolves. It begins at sundown and runs on into the night, with the first few hours of darkness often affording the most action.

Right now, water temperature is not a factor to the bass and when they will feed, because it's perfect and will undoubtedly hold for a while. Their main concern becomes sunlight. During the early spring they could put up with it, since it meant heat and extra power for their "metabolic motors." Now, bright sunlight is just a steadily increasing hindrance that announces their presence to food and enemies. It's avoided, if possible.

This isn't the only reason darker hours become the bass' major feeding time. Crayfish, a highly nutritional and favorite food of the bass, come out after sundown to browse the lake bottom and make themselves conveniently available for dinner. Also, on many lakes and ponds, daylight becomes synonymous with heavy angling pressure and other similar disturbances. It doesn't take most adult bass long to realize that a feeding excursion to the shallows will be more successful if postponed until after hours.

I would guess the major reason the first hours of darkness are better is simply because the bass don't wish to wait any longer to feed. With the relatively unfavorable conditions — and therefore limited feeding — of the daylight hours, most bass are more than ready to crunch a few crayfish and baitfish when dusk finally rolls in. Also, the shallows are still quite warm and rich in oxygen from daytime's sun, and waiting to feed at midnight would mean encountering slightly less favorable conditions — and at 4 a.m. a little worse yet.

In the final stages of this late spring period a secondary prime time begins to develop in the morning. With the now-ideal water temperature comes an increase in the bass' digestion rate, which means they must feed more than ever. For example, studies have shown that a bass digests his food twice as fast and eats twice as much in 72-degree water as he does in 65. In terms of hours, this breaks down to mean a full stomach will be practically empty again in 12 hours in 72-degree water. So, assuming a bass has a good feed at say 9 p.m., his stomach should be banging on the kitchen door again by nine the next morning. I don't know if this thoroughly explains why a mid-morning prime time occurs, but the fact remains it does quite often, as evidenced by the personal accounts of many anglers across the country.

This period comes to a screeching halt when the shallows reach a certain temperature. In my area of southeast Iowa it happens right about 77 degrees. In northern regions it will usually be lower, and in the south higher. Whatever it is, it ends the good run of early night fishing, because for the first time of the year the shallows have become too warm for the big bass. The spawning is pretty much over now, so most bass change their feeding times to the next period.

SUMMER PRIME TIMES

At the very beginning, prime time will run from first light to early morning. Again, its timing is due to water temperature. While dusk's shallows are now too warm for feeding, during the night some of this heat can be lost to the air, making dawn the coolest time of day. For a short time, depending on the weather, the upper layers at daybreak should be back within the bass' optimum, granting them a few more days of major feeding at this food-filled depth. But little by little the heat gained during the day will outweigh the heat lost at night, and the lunkers will slowly be forced downward, bringing an end to the good spring fishing.

Hello summer doldrums! Despite the fact that bass eat more in warmer water, summer fishing can be very tough at times. Before the spawning season, conditions were excellent for catching bass. The food supply was at its lowest of the year, making any lure look exceedingly delicious. The bass were starved from the long winter's fast. The oxygen was plentiful for any activity. About the only negative factor was the relatively cold water that left the fish a little sluggish. Now, in the bad old summertime, the water is too warm, the oxygen sometimes too poor, the bass' fat supply replenished and your chunk of plastic is competing with the real thing — billions of real things!

Chances are you won't find any prime times *per se*. One hour could be just as good (or poor) as the next. Especially in structureless waters, the bass as a rule may be concentrated in only a few areas — such as off shallow points or on bends of submerged creek channels. If you can find them and have patience, good fishing may be yours. I've found that such a school usually turns on approximately every two hours. You catch two or three in about as many minutes, then spend the next 120 minutes envying water skiers. At least two brief migrations to

120

the medium depths may occur each day, but any major movements are usually reserved for those low-light hours. Dawn should be a little better than dusk, with the water being its coolest of the 24 hours. Late summer trophies are hard to come by, but if that's your desire, keep going at night.

Finally summer breaks and water temperatures begin to drop. During the last few weeks of this period, water conditions fluctuate so rapidly that feeding times are virtually impossible to predict. Having been locked in thermal stratification for months, the upper layers are now more uniform, better oxygenated and cooler. Until the shallows cool down to, and then below, the optimum 70-75-degree range, the pattern is pretty much where and when you find it. But once one is discovered it should hold until the next weather change.

FALL PRIME TIMES

As the water temperature drops below 70 degrees, it again becomes the major factor in predicting prime times. And the cooler it gets, the more important it is. This is the time of year bass can go on feeding frenzies, and your entire catch may come from a frantic 30-minute stretch.

It's much like the early spring period, in that bass choose the heat of the day for feeding. The only difference is that in the fall the water is normally warmest around noon, while spring's hottest hour falls during mid-afternoon. (Explaining just why this is could put us both to sleep.) So, on those sunny days center your time around the 10 a.m. to 2 p.m. hours and be prepared for some short but fast action. If it's cloudy, the occurrence of a prime time is less likely.

SUMMARY

For quick reference, the general pattern of prime times throughout the year is listed at the conclusion of this chapter. As you apply this information to your fishing, please keep in mind that no long-range fishing forecast, regardless of its foundation, can ever claim total accuracy. There are too many unpredictable variables, the most important of which has to be *hunger*. If all the bass in a lake became hungry and started to feed at the same time, we could foretell the next feeding period to within minutes just by calculating their digestion rates in that particular water temperature. But they don't — and that sure complicates things.

Fortunately, even starved bass are often kept from entering a positive feeding mood by adverse water conditions. Either from instinct or experience they know that any attempt would prove futile, so they wait until the odds turn in their favor. That is the basis of this "prime time" system.

As you're coming onto the water at the beginning of a prime time, and a friend with a huge string of bass tells you they were hitting like crazy two hours ago, or a suggested prime time finds the bass so turned off you'd think the lake was experiencing a power failure, don't get discouraged. Over the long run, the man who fishes these prime times consistently will stand head and shoulders above anyone who doesn't.

TEMPERATURE AT 3-5 FEET	PRIME TIME(S)	SECONDARY
Up to 55	Noon to 4 p.m. On Sunny days	
56 to 60	Noon to 2 p.m.	Mid-morning & Late afternoon
61 to 69	9 a.m. to 5 p.m. For non-spawners 5 p.m. to 8 p.m. For spawners	Early Night
70 to 76	Early night	Mid-morning
77 to 80	First light To mid-morning	Most other times For small bass
81 on up	Pre-dawn & night	Dusk and Most other times
70 on down	10 a.m. to 2 p.m.	

Figure 32

PART THREE
GUIDE TO THE SEASONS

The arrival and departure of the various bass fishing seasons mean different dates on the calendar to different fishermen. In late March, for example, a Texan could find 55-degree water and hungry bass, while to his Minnesota cousin that same date may mean guarding his hothouse from reckless snowmobilers. Consequently, no day-by-day guide to bass fishing can be based on a calendar and still be accurate.

Water temperature is still a much better indicator. While a number of environmental factors are responsible for changes in bass behavior, this one is usually the most important. And it's certainly the easiest to monitor. For these reasons, the following *"Guide to the Seasons"* is organized by degrees, rather than dates.

Please keep in mind that when a specific water temperature is given — such as those heading various sections of the following chapter — it is referring to the general temperature of the shallows (unless otherwise specified). And by "shallows" we will mean approximately *three to ten feet*, the usual location of feeding bass.

124

Chapter 11
Early Spring
Water: Up to 55 Degrees

Regardless of your area, early spring bass fishing normally begins when a good warming trend puts the kiss of death on winter and raises the water temperature a few degrees for the first time that year. In the far north this may not happen until late April and begins with water barely reading 38 degrees. In the southern extremes — excluding Florida and the desert southwest — it can occur as early as late January and have a water temperature already in the 50's.

The end of this period, however, is basically the same everywhere. It comes as the water nears the high 50's and the bass' fancies turn to thoughts of spawning.

We'll start by listing the general, yet very important factors which hold true for all bass (regardless of region or climate) throughout this entire early spring period. These not only offer helpful insights into successful bass fishing, they lay the foundation for the more specialized, temperature-by-temperature guide that follows in this and proceeding chapters.

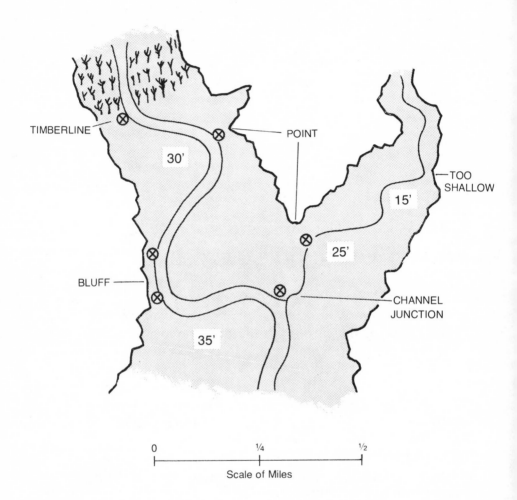

Figure 33. *During winter, bass normally school around a particular object or structure in relatively deep water, connected to the shallows by a short, well-defined travel route. The presence of creek channels simplifies the search, as they are a favorite bass structure. NOTE: The channel junction shown above rates only as a "possible winter home" because it may be too far (¼ mile) from the nearest shallow water.*

LOCATING THE BASS

Below are the key features bass find desirable in selecting a location during this time. You may not always find spots containing all of these, but the more one has, the better it should be, particularly in terms of lunkers.

Deep Water. While most success seems to come from the shallows in spring, some anglers fare well working the depths. A lot depends on the particular lake and your familiarity with it. The problem with fishing deep is that if you don't score, you can't be certain whether it was your failure to find the bass or their lack of interest. Fish digest their food slowly (two to four days) in cold water, so feeding spells are few and far between. And just the fact the bass are deep hints they aren't too keen on eating. In lakes and ponds with a good population, if you catch one bass from a deep-water area, you may take a lot more.

If you want to tackle the deep, think in terms of finding the bass' winter homes. These are almost always where deep water comes close to shallow feeding grounds and the two are connected by a well-defined travel route. Examples are where a creek channel swings in against a rock bluff or point, or where it intersects with another channel or treeline running directly to the shallows. (See Figure 33.) The exact depth of these winter homes will vary from lake to lake, but as a rule of thumb start first with the deepest water in the area.

Shallow Water. In most situations you'll do better concentrating on the shallows. The reason is because a shallow bass is usually a feeding bass and therefore more willing to snap your lure. It's also easier to find his holding areas, since many of the structures can be seen with the naked eye. Those shallow areas adjacent to the bass' deep-water winter homes are often the earliest spring producers. They are the first feeding grounds hungry bass come to upon breaking the long winter fast. As the water warms farther, they will spread to more distant areas. (See Figure 34.)

Good Cover. The shallower a bass comes, and the bigger he is, the more important concealment is to him. Lunkers must

NEWLY FALLEN TREES

LARGE, SHALLOW STUMPS

WEEDS

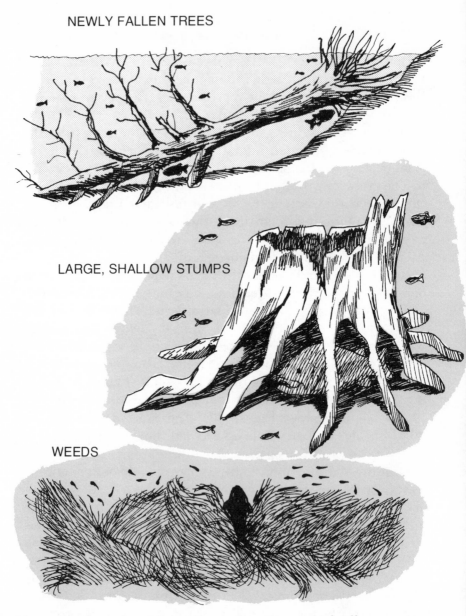

Figure 34. Examples of Prime Cover. Structures which offer cover to both bass and prey are the best, especially for lunkers. However, the object should be on or very near a major travel route of the baitfish.

rely almost entirely on ambushing, since in a fin race with baitfish they'd be outmaneuvered. Any object that offers camouflage and a quick exit is potentially bassworthy.

However, the best ones are those which also provide cover to the bass' prey and are on a major travel route of those baitfish. Smaller fish need protective cover the same as bass. Ideally, these are dense masses of sticks or weeds with numerous openings large enough for the baitfish, but too small for most predators. Bass love to camp nearby, because the minute one of these morsels gets careless, dinner is but a short burst away. One of the best examples of this type of structure is a freshly fallen shoreline tree. The thin bushy branches protect the baitfish, while the thick limbs or trunk harbors the bass. Other examples would be a large brushpile, a tree or stump with an exposed root system, or any large object in or near weeds.

Travel Routes of the Baitfish. Even the most ideal cover will be worthless to a hungry bass if it isn't on or near a major travel route of his prey. This can be the shoreline, a long weedline, treeline or brushline, a shallow creek channel or any well-defined structure(s) that help small fish move from one place to another. The shoreline is usually the most travelled, because it always rings the entire body of water and it's found where the baitfish prefer to be — the extreme shallows. It also has merit in its ease of detection by most fishermen. But in lakes and ponds heavy with vegetation, the weedline would be better with its additional offer of concealment to the baitfish. (See Figure 35.)

Underfished Areas. If there's one thing that can throw a wrench in the works, it's too much fishing pressure. This has become a real problem in most bass waters today, and smarter fishermen treat it as one of the most critical variables. Bass, especially old-timers, dislike setting up house in places repeatedly disturbed by their enemies above. And those that do anyway probably have learned to button their lips or skulk away at the first sign of invasion. Therefore, you may be wise to

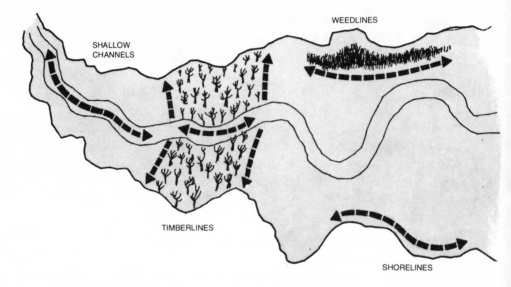

SHALLOW
CHANNELS

WEEDLINES

TIMBERLINES

SHORELINES

Figure 35. The best of cover is worthless to a hungry bass if it is not near a baitfish travel route. Above are some of the baitfish's favorite routes.

spend less time hitting the well-known, obvious structures and more time searching out virgin territory.

Warm Water Areas. Certain parts of a medium-to-large lake usually warm faster, thereby providing better bass fishing in the early spring. The logical theory is that baitfish, which may be scarce now, congregate in these pockets, because plankton (their food) is more abundant. That congregation draws the bass, as does the warmer water itself.

Warm areas are easy to find, because they are nearly always along the northern shorelines. The heating rays of the sun strike longest and hardest here. And the predominantly southerly wind pushes the lake's warm upper layers to the north end. However, since baitfish try to avoid strong currents, your best bet is to hit those coves and cuts with some protection from the immediate wind. (See Figure 36.)

130

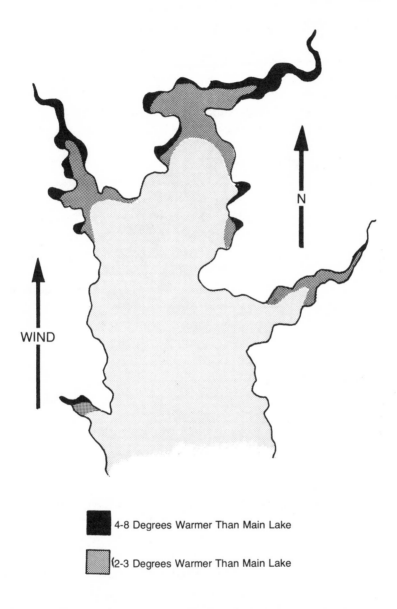

4-8 Degrees Warmer Than Main Lake

(2-3 Degrees Warmer Than Main Lake

Figure 36. Warm Water Areas in Early Spring. The combination of southerly winds and sunshine can quicky warm the water along north shorelines, particularly in sheltered coves and cuts.

THE BEST TIMES TO FISH

There is no question that certain days, as well as certain times of any given day, are better than others for catching bass. While there are a number of known factors influencing the feeding moods of these fish, the most dominant appears to be the weather and its direct effect on water conditions. This subject was covered thoroughly in Chapters 9 and 10, so we will just review the highlights here.

Bass are much more active in the spring, if the water is *warming* — particularly in the first five feet. That is the primary rule. Being cold-blooded, a fish's activity is vastly dependent on the temperature of his surroundings. Warming water acts as a stimulus, firing up his metabolism and urging him to feed, while cooling water does the opposite.

At the very least, the water temperature should be holding steady after a period of warming.

The first exceptional warming trend of spring will hold a high lunker potential throughout, because it stimulates fish for the first time in many months.

A day with a sharp rise in water temperature will be better than one with a gradual rise, due to the greater stimulus in a shorter time.

The first day of a good warming trend is usually the best because the stimulus is sudden.

A couple days of warm sunny weather, followed by a sudden overcast, is often super.

On the other hand, sunny, calm days can be good, especially during early spring. With a calm surface, the sun can warm the shallows as much as ten degrees, creating a layer of heaven for fish.

The heat-of-the-day period from about 10 a.m. to 4 p.m. is usually the best time to go for bass. This is especially true on sunny days in lakes with at least average cover. If a hungry bass cannot find objects to sufficiently conceal him in the sun-brightened shallows of mid-day, he may wait until evening or night to feed there.

132

The Basics of Weather's Effect on Water. The sun, wind and air temperature are the main factors producing changes in water temperature. Anytime the air is warmer than the water, the latter will experience a rise in temperature — the degree depending on how much warmer the air is. Without wind to mix the two, however, the rise will be minor. The longer and more directly the sun strikes the water, the more of its heat will be absorbed into the upper layers. Wave action hampers heat penetration by reflecting and scattering the sun's rays.

LURE SELECTION

Without a doubt, the best lure for a bass in cold water is one that almost bumps his nose. It should be something you can manipulate right into where a bass is thought to be. If, for example, the object is a brushpile, try a lure that will fall through it without hanging up, such as a spinnerbait or plastic worm. Some anglers claim the latter isn't effective in cold water. Others, including myself, disagree.

You also want a lure you can work slowly. This makes it seem like easier prey and induces more strikes. Try using a spinnerbait with large blades and a trailer or a plastic worm with a small slip sinker. If the structure permits, a crankbait retrieved just fast enough to activate its proper action can also be good. As the water warms, the speed can be increased.

It is generally advised to start with smaller lures in cold water. I can give no factual explanation why, other than most anglers agree to their effectiveness. As for color, the best advice is no advice. There is just too much disagreement among bass fishermen to offer any concrete answers. I'm certain this is because a bass' diet varies with season, region, position in a lake and his particular situation. One exception is that you should find white or fluorescent colors better in murky waters, due to their increased visibility. But even then don't hesitate to experiment. Sooner or later the bass will tell you the right color(s).

The technique to employ in early spring is *casting accuracy*.

If you find what seems to be a likely hideout for Ol' Maude, spray it with casts. Go over it, around it, through it and under it. Hit every square inch. If the target is shallow, try to cast past it at least 10 feet, so the splash doesn't frighten the fish. Then bring it back right against the object. In water this cold, a bass won't even consider a lure unless it's in easy striking distance.

Since the food supply is lowest of the year, a hungry bass will hit just about anything. Instead of choosing a lure you think the bass will like, concentrate more on matching it to the situation. It should first go where and do what you want it to. The bass themselves will guide you from there.

BASS FISHING BY WATER TEMPERATURE

Now that we've covered the basics of early spring, we'll see how to go after bass in the various water temperatures.

36 to 39 Degrees (North Only). In most cases only those waters that ice up each winter will be this cold in early spring. These temperatures usually last no longer than the ice chunks themselves. Most fishermen believe it's ridiculous to go for bass under these conditions, but the truth is the action can be quite good, if done correctly and at the right time.

Larry Kauffman of Kalona, Iowa first alerted me to the fact that bass up to 14 inches could be taken by casting a Number 3 Mepps Spinner onto the ice chunks near shore, then dropping it off the edge. I did poorly at first, then in the following years, I discovered that the secret was to be there on the first day the ice began breaking up and at mid-day. Other times provided little more than casting exercise.

The initial opening up of the water after months of isolation from the atmosphere stimulates most life forms within. Fresh and often badly-needed oxygen is suddenly drawn into the water, as is heat from the sun and air. A few species of plankton become more abundant near the surface, calling small baitfish up to feed, which in turn attracts a few bass. Lunkers, however, seem hard to come by yet.

134

40 to 49 Degrees: Lunkertime. When water temperatures are in the 40's, you may fish all day to catch one bass, but odds are it will be a good one. If the water is warming, the lunkers will be stirring. With their winter fat virtually depleted, one by one they'll lumber toward the shallows in search of a desperately needed meal.

The "pecking order" is in full swing now. This means the largest fish will usually occupy the best locations, even if they must run smaller ones out. The next best spot will hold the next largest fish, and so on down the line. If you seek out the prime areas, then be patient, you may hang your best bass of the year.

Possibly the best tactic to use is to fish during the warming trends. Bass are very touchy in 40-49-degree water, responding favorably when it warms and negatively when it cools. A "nice" day invariably brings at least a few lunkers to the shallows, and that's where your chances are the greatest.

I recommend first those warm pockets along the northern shores. If it's the first warming trend of the year, concentrate mostly on main lake features adjacent to the bass' winter homes. These are the first places bass stop, as they begin their spring migration to the shallows. As the water continues warming, they spread to more distant areas. (See Figure 37.)

On sunny days the back end of a sheltered cove or cut can be five degrees warmer than the main lake just a few hundred yards away. This will attract baitfish and hold them — and that means bass. How many and how large depends on the quality of cover. Remember that if a structure offers concealment to both bass and baitfish, is on a major travel route such as the shoreline or weedline, and if it hasn't been voted your local bass club's favorite casting target for the third year in a row, it could easily hold a lunker. For just these reasons, newly-fallen trees are often ideal. So are those unobvious brushpiles, stumps and trees that can be found only with a depth-finder or deep-running lure. Resting in slightly deeper water, these will be overlooked by 95 percent of the fishermen, making them worth finding in heavily fished areas.

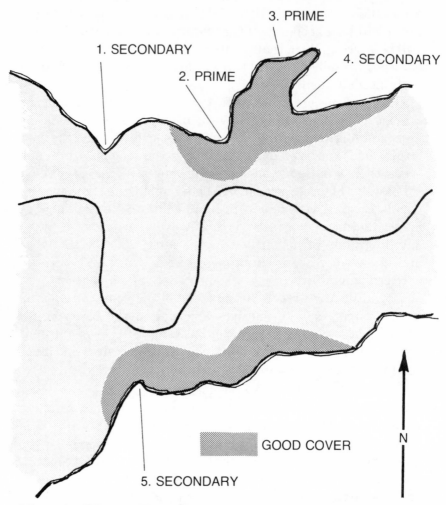

Figure 37. Why Are These Areas Labeled As They Are? Point 1 rates only as Secondary (and a poor one at that), because it lacks cover in a region with plenty. Point 2 is Prime because it has everything to attract bass – cover, nearby channel, a clear travel route from deep water to the shallows and is on the warmer north shore. Early spring bass would move first to this point, then later into the adjacent cove. Point 4 lacks only having the channel swing in close. Point 5 is very close to being Prime, but is on the cooler south shore.

136

Secondary Structures. In the long run, fishing just the prime areas will produce the best results. But since no two days, bass or bodies of water are exactly the same, there may be times when these surrender little or nothing. Now you are faced with the age-old angler's dilemma: "Do I stick it out here and hope the bass move in or do I take off and try other places?"

In 40-49-degree water the answer lies in the bass population of your water, then in how willing you are to settle for smaller fish. In lakes with a poor population you'll usually find that if the prime areas produce nothing, then neither will the secondary ones. On the other hand, when there's an abundance of bass, competition among them is so strong you can often take smaller ones off any good or even fair structure. You may even luck into a lunker.

Secondary structures are labelled such because although potentially quite good, they fall just one or two ingredients short of being prime. For example, you may find an ideal brushpile offering excellent concealment to both bass and bait. It's located near the shoreline, a major travel route of the baitfish, and adjacent to deep water, providing easy access for bass just coming up from their winter homes. But instead of being in a warm pocket along a north shore, it's on a main lake point in the southern end. That's a "secondary structure" and is certainly worth fishing. True, warm pockets are better, but are by no means mandatory.

You may find one of those perfect-looking points jutting out into the lake with a quick drop to deep water on at least one side. The best way to determine its potential quickly is to scan it with your depth-finder, then take a look around you, or at an accurate map. If that lake has a well-defined channel, you know the point will be much better if that channel swings in close. If the lake lacks good cover and you found signs of weeds or brush there, you may have hit the mother lode. Then again, if you notice some flooded timber beginning just a hundred yards away, that point may harbor small schoolies at best.

The examples could go on and on, but I'm sure you get the

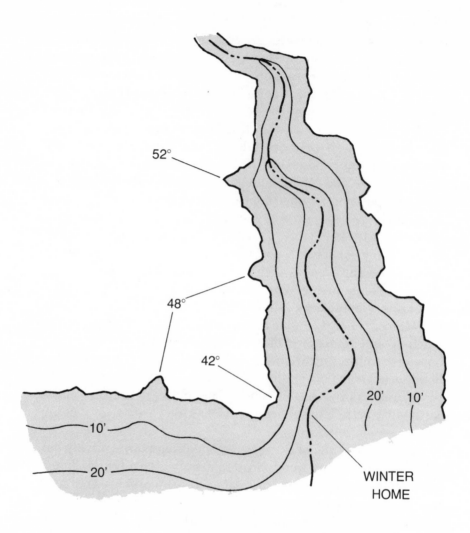

Figure 38. Horizontal Movements. In this situatin, once the water starts warming in early spring, bass begin leaving the deep-water winter home and move vertically up the steeper side of the point. Then, as the warming continues there will be a gradual, horizontal migration . . .mostly toward the upper end of the arm. Here, their main travel route would be the shoreline, and any structure along it would be worth fishing. Good cover in either of the cuts would be ideal.

138

idea. Besides, all you have to remember are the basic preferences for bass we covered earlier in this chapter. Then make up your own list of examples. I promise you that will make you a much better fisherman than simply following the pointed finger of someone else.

50 TO 55 DEGREES: INCREASING ACTION.

There isn't much change as water temperature pushes into the 50s. One major difference, however, is that the warmer water has brought many more bass to within range of your hook. This means trophy possibilities should be even better, providing angling pressure hasn't been too severe. Plus, now you will hang some smaller bass, too.

If your sights are strictly on big bass, continue fishing the prime areas and times. If you prefer stalking bass of all sizes for more strikes per hour, you may wish to spend some time on the easier-to-find secondary structures.

Horizontal Movements. You'll discover that in general the bass have migrated farther from their wintering areas and scattered to a few more shallow sections. How far they have pushed will depend on how much the water has warmed above its winter normalcy. (See Figure 38.)

In the above example, the logical location of the bass' winter home is where depicted, because it offers both deep water (30-35 feet) and a short travel route to the shallows. During the first one or two warming trends of the spring, you may find that immediate point the best fishing. As the water continues to warm, some of those bass will begin a more horizontal movement into shallower areas close by, such as either of the two cuts shown, and later around the small bay upstream. The best tactic to use is to calculate the migration route(s) then fish those structures which provide a good stopping place. In this situation (assuming the area is devoid of brush, timber or weedlines) the logical route is from the steeper side of that main point, up the arm via the shoreline.

Chapter 12
Late Spring
Water: 56 to 78 Degrees

In early spring, the bass fishing generally improved each week. Once found, the basic patterns pretty well held. Now, in the late spring, things slowly begin changing. The once predominant desire of most bass to feed gradually gives way to the more deeply-rooted instinct to spawn. This is a time of transition for bass and different game plans for the angler.

56 TO 60 DEGREES (PRE-NESTING)

For the most part, in water this temperature you should continue fishing the same as the previous weeks. Key on those warm sunny days, as they raise the water temperature and the bass' spirits. In fact, the sudden appearance of the sun on an otherwise cloudy day is commonly instrumental in turning the bass on. Steadily warming water will also mean more and better feeding periods, plus more bass showing up in that perfect angling depth of 10 feet or less. The word buzzing around marinas and tackle stores about now is: "The bass are biting!"

140

While the egg-laden females remain cautious and relatively scattered at all depths, the males begin to cruise the shallows. With one eye out for a suitable nesting location and the other for something edible, they travel the two-to-six-foot depths along the sides of coves and other wind-sheltered but sunny areas with gradual slopes. As this depth passes 56 degrees in the north and 60 in the south, one-by-one the males home in on a particular area and settle down to some serious nest-building. Lure-wise, there still is not enough food in the water to make the bass selective, so anything working temptingly within striking distance should do the trick. As for the best time of day, it's still 10 a.m. to 3 p.m. But don't be afraid to try dawn and dusk.

61 TO 65 DEGREES (NESTING)

By the time the temperature at three to six feet hits approximately 61 degrees in the north and 65 in the south, the nesting season is well under way for the males. The female pattern changes little, if any. As it can be the most beneficial to key on these nesters, let's see what they look for in a spawning area.

A firm clean bottom or structure. Soft mushy areas, such as decayed vegetation and silt, are poor nesting grounds because the decomposition taking place there uses up much of the oxygen the eggs need, and because the eggs could not adhere securely to them. In waters where "muck" coats the entire bottom, bass eggs have been observed attached to branches of brushpiles as much as three feet off the bottom — proving the adaptability of this marvelous fish.

Ample sunshine. For proper incubation, eggs need strong sunlight much of the day, such as along northern shores. In most lakes this cannot be achieved much below five or six feet, so your search should be confined to this depth or shallower. It is interesting to note, however, that in Lake Mead, one of the world's clearest bodies of water, some bass were seen spawning at a depth of 25 feet.

PRIME SPAWNING AREAS

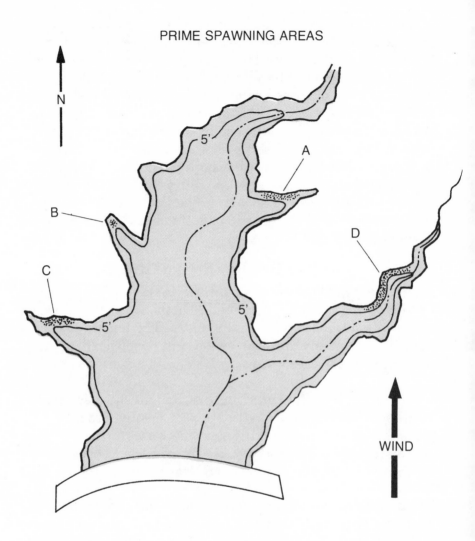

Figure 39. "A" and "C" are the best areas to start looking. Each is a north shoreline protected from strong south winds of spring. "A" may be the better, as a key migration route (the channlel) swings close by. The north shore of "B" will probably have too much wave action, so only the back end of the cove is prime. The only problem with "D" is that it is in a live creek cove and too much current and/or silt may wash in after rains.

Nearby cover. Once the eggs hatch, they need some kind of cover to protect them from predators.

Little or no current. Too much current can jar the eggs loose or cover them with silt. This is why main lake shorelines and coves with live creeks or constant boat traffic are usually devoid of nests.

If your water is clear enough, there is no better or faster way of locating nesting bass than to ease along the shoreline on foot or in a boat, visually spotting them. They may scoot away as you approach, but will shortly return. In murky water use a stick or paddle to probe the bottom for firmness — pea gravel is ideal, even with a few inches of silt over it since the bass can usually fan the sediment away. However you do it, begin with sheltered coves or bays either on the north side of the lake or with a good north shore in itself.

Once the bass are found, most conventional methods will hook them. You can expect solid hits, as the males are quite aggressive now, and the lures can be worked at faster speeds. Plastic worms seem preferable, followed by spinnerbaits, then crankbaits. But this order is far from rigid.

66 TO 72 DEGREES (EGG LAYING AND PROTECTION)

Once that five-to-six-foot level reaches the high 60s in the north and the low 70s in the south and holds there on into a full moon, the actual spawning ritual begins. Each male will try seducing a cruising female to his nest to unload some of her roe. Once done, she may stay around for a few days to help with sentry duty, or she may shuttle her fickle self off to "lay" with at least one other male.

The male will stay on the bed with the eggs or fry anywhere from one week to a little over two, depending on what the water temperature does. A rapid rise can hatch the eggs in three days, while a slight cooling may prolong the blessed event for over a week. On the other hand, a sharp drop in the temperature, a marked rise or fall of the water level, an influx of dirty water such as after a heavy rain, or the presence of too many

hungry panfish (a real problem in many lakes and ponds) can spell disaster for the spawn by either killing the eggs outright or forcing the male to abandon the nest.

If the bass fishing suddenly goes sour, spawning is probably the reason. Both sexes feed little at this time. About the only way to take a spawner during the day is to work a plastic worm, jig-and-eel or spinnerbait right into the nest. If the bass feels it's a threat to his wards, he may gingerly carry it a few feet away from the nest. A moving line may be your only clue to a pick-up, and you must strike hard and fast. If you do catch one, give some serious thought to throwing it back immediately, because an unguarded batch of young can be wiped out in no time by bluegills or crappies. A scraggly-looking bass with a bloody tail is the mark of a protecting parent.

Not all bass spawn at the same time. In fact, the entire period may be stretched over two or more months. When a noticeable lag does occur in the bassing action, it does not mean *all* the bass are spawning, just a high percentage. It's conceivable that half the population is still actively feeding and vulnerable to your hook. Consequently, you may be wise to forego the spawning beds in favor of those more typical patterns that were catching bass during the previous weeks. It's difficult to leave an area where you can see four and five-pounders looming nonchalantly under your feet, but the odds are against catching them, at least during the daylight hours.

Try Night Fishing. If there is a "secret" to taking bass, especially big bass, during late spring and summer, night fishing has to be it. The majority of bass anglers — even the fanatics — close their ears to this suggestion, simply because it's very difficult for them to get out at this time. They'd rather stick with the more conventional hours than come in from the pond at midnight to find the wife and kids have moved.

Look at the situation this creates: An average lake on an average day is loaded with fishermen, skiers, swimmers, etc., all competing for outdoor fun and quite possibly spooking the hell out of most bass. But come nightfall, the water is calm, quiet and the sole property of any man who wants it. And from the bass' viewpoint this is certainly a more amiable time to go shopping in the shallows.

Actually, bass will feed at night for better reasons. Their sensitive "night vision" affords them a strong visual edge over most baitfish, which have none. And because the prey is virtually blind at this time, they often congregate in vast schools in the shallows. This offers security to the individual, but makes the group, as a whole, easy prey.

Even more important, at night bass find their favorite food in greatest abundance. Having incredibly poor eyesight in any light, the nutritious crayfish stay hidden in rocks and mud burrows during the day. Then under cover of darkness they squirt out to forage the bottom for food. Most wiley old bass know where the good crabbing grounds are, and that with patience, stealth and a superior night vision, the crayfish will be easy pickings.

Finally, bass often feed at night because they simply get hungry. Once the water temperature passes the high 60's, bass' metabolism starts operating at full throttle, so frequent nourishment is required. How often they will enter a positive feeding mood is hard to say, but an educated guess would be at least once every three hours. Night or day makes little difference to a bass' stomach, since the sun never shines there anyway.

The case is slightly different with the spawners. True, post-dusk is a good time to catch them, too, but the hours of later afternoon to twilight are generally better. Theory has it that when the sun is heavy on the nests, bass have no interest in feeding, only in protecting their grounds. Once that sun diminishes, however, the spawning instinct gives way somewhat to an empty stomach. They'll still nail anything invading their nest, but now it's for their own sake as much as the children's.

EVALUATING YOUR LAKE'S NIGHT POTENTIAL

Clear water: good night fishing.
Dirty water: good-night, fish!

During the day, sunlight can penetrate deeply into clear water, making the bass quite visible to their prey at almost any depth. So, any attempt to answer a stomach's call would be met with marginal success at best. A smarter bass will simply bide his time until sundown brings him the visual edge.

In dirty water, there is rarely a visual edge, night or day. The billions of tiny silt or algae particles can cut visibility down to zero even during the brightest hours. Since a bass here would rely mostly on his other senses (hearing, smelling, vibration detection) for feeding, the lightless hours would offer no additional advantage.

146

Few people fish for bass at night, which is just one of many reasons it's such an effective technique.

Most waters rank somewhere between clear and dirty, and frequently seesaw back and forth. In water of this type it's important to know its *average clarity*. If it's clearer than normal, you may find the night bassing to be 24-karat dynamite, because the unusually bright waters of daytime can greatly restrict a bass' efforts to indulge, bringing him to sundown with a lean and hungry look. Clean water would also allow him to see better than usual at night.

If water is dirtier than normal, a bass' most active feeding may take place during daylight, because he can't see for beans, regardless of the sun's position. The problem with lakes having clarity fluctuations is that a sudden algae bloom or heavy rain can destroy fantastic night fishing in a fraction of the time it took to create it. As a rule of thumb, don't put too much stock in night fishing unless you can see a lure a foot or more below the surface during the day.

NIGHT TECHNIQUES

There's nothing complicated about fishing at night, since the only major difference between it and daytime is that the bass and you cannot see quite as well. With that in mind, let logic be your guide. If you like plastic worms, use at least the six-inch size, go to a smaller weight and work the rig slowly. This gives your quarry more time to zero in. With a spinnerbait, use large blades and a slow, steady retrieve. In my experience, surface baits and gurgling spinners are the most fun to fish, and they do catch bass. But the majority of lunkers seem to come when I cast parallel and close to the shoreline, then work the lure slowly along the bottom through good cover.

If the moon has a role in what nights you go for bass, nobody's pinned it down conclusively thus far. It's effect apparently rests on the more demonstrative variables, such as region, climate, current weather and lake condition. There is, however, enough agreement among some experts to warrant the following suggestion: The five or so nights before a full moon are usually the best, with each night bettering the one before.

148

Why? The explanations range from gravitational pull to astrology. Personally, I just say it's the extra illumination, then quickly change the subject.

73 TO 78 DEGREES (POST-SPAWNING)

Some spawning will still be going on, even after the water reaches 80 degrees. But for all practical purposes it's over, and along with it that so-called "good spring fishing." The spawned-out females and battered males limp away from the nesting grounds to recuperate in deeper water. You'd think they'd go on feeding rampages to make up for lost time, but most have neither the strength nor the tail to run anything down.

The shallow water bass fisherman may still pick up a few late spawners or dinks too young to mate. But the talk now is that the bass have turned off, so most anglers do the same. This isn't necessarily the case. The bass have only moved and are somewhat restricted in their lure-chasing capabilities. By changing your thinking 180 degrees and laying in a fresh supply of patience, you can cash in on what everybody else is leaving behind.

Forget the shallows and look for those deep-water resting areas. By definition, these will be *objects* such as submerged trees and brushpiles, or configurations of land, such as points, breaklines, dropoffs and channel banks, that are close and connected to the spawning grounds by well-defined travel routes.

If, for example, you had been taking spawners along the side of a particular cove, move out and work the deeper water of the point. If there's a sunken brushpile directly adjacent to these spawning areas and in relatively deep water, try it. If on the bank there's a fallen tree whose top end is submerged in at least 10 feet of water, a resting lunker could easily be there. Anchor about a cast away from these suspected hangouts and work every square foot meticulously and slowly with a variety of lures. If nothing comes up in about 10 minutes, leave the area and try again in about an hour. Don't give up on a likely spot until you've hit it three or four times. Even then, try it again a few days later.

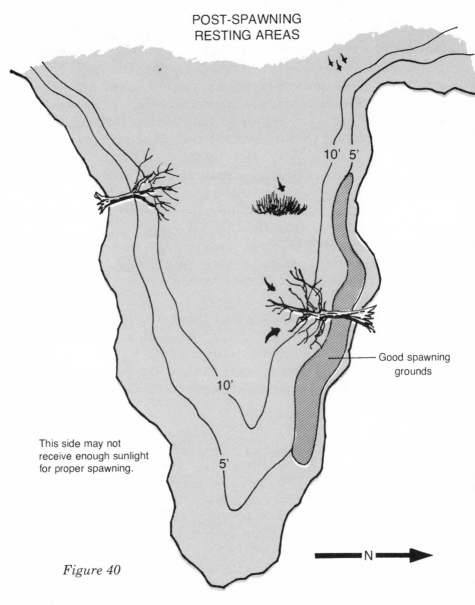

POST-SPAWNING
RESTING AREAS

10' 5'

Good spawning
grounds

10'

This side may not
receive enough sunlight
for proper spawning.

5'

N →

Figure 40

Chapter 13
Summer
Water: Stratified

In past months the bass followed one or two basic patterns of behavior, which varied little for weeks. Now you may find three or four patterns at the same time, each no more stable than the weather. As the water is well stratified thermally, temperature — with structure and possibly oxygen — has a great deal to do with regulating the bass' depth, enabling the scientific angler to often pinpoint the fish vertically. To do the same horizontally, on the other hand, seldom requires more than a working knowledge of your lake's structure, plus a dash of flexibility and exploration.

There are always special "tricks" to taking bass during the summer, but the best is simply to pay close attention to the basics.

EARLY SUMMER

On most lakes, early summer offers a lot of action to all types of bass fishermen. The veteran begins pulling limits from his favorite hole. The novice finds welcome success plugging the shoreline with lures he never thought would work. Even the minnow-dunking crappie angler is treated to an occasional "fighter" at the end of his four-pound test. Virtually every healthy bass in the lake will enter a positive feeding mood at least two times during a typical day.

Roughly two weeks after the termination of spawning duties, a bass is healed, rejuvenated and ready for some serious food ingestion. By now the temperature in the shallows has been at least 75 degrees for a couple weeks, which should be your signal to switch to a summertime fishing pattern. Some bass will take up residence in shallow cover until the water gets too warm. Some will prefer roaming the shallows, bouncing from one prime feeding area to the next. Others, especially in water short on shallow cover, will school near key feeding grounds.

A SAMPLE SITUATION

Figure 41 illustrates a typical profile of an early summer lake. To find the pattern(s) your bass will be using, simply run down the checklist of important variables. In this example they will read out as follows:

Water Temperature. You can look for schooling or resting bass around the nine to ten-foot level, because here they find their ideal temperature of 72-73 degrees. You can also expect active feeding in the shallows, as this region's temperature is still well within the tolerance range.

Oxygen. This should not be a factor this early.

Light. With the sunlight penetrating this deeply (25 feet) it's almost a guarantee that larger bass at least will use the dark and semi-dark hours for major feeding.

Food. If present, crayfish should be the bass' main diet now. These crustaceans prefer the shallow, rocky, weedy areas and forage mostly at night. The recent spawn has also generated an abundance of foodfish fry, which will hang almost exclusively in these same areas, plus brushpiles, when available.

152

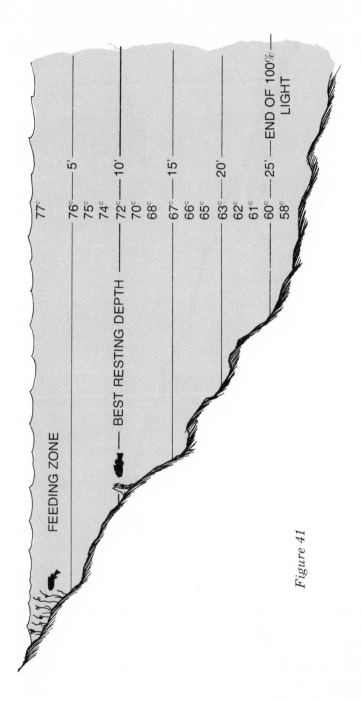

FEEDING ZONE

BEST RESTING DEPTH

77°
76° — 5'
75°
74°
72° — 10'
70°
68°
67° — 15'
66°
65°
63° — 20'
62°
61°
60° — 25' — END OF 100% LIGHT
58°

Figure 41

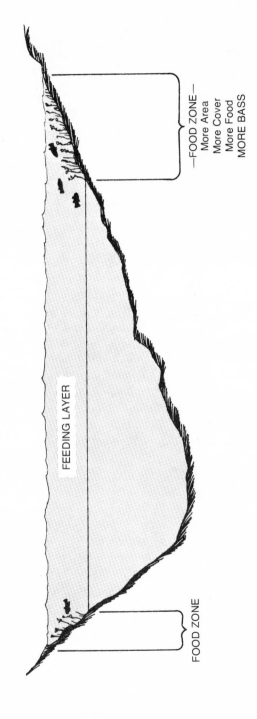

FOOD ZONE — More Area More Cover More Food MORE BASS

FEEDING LAYER

FOOD ZONE

Figure 42. Bass prefer gradual slopes in the warm months, and often roam laterally along them.

Structure. Many bass will be scattered in the shallows around the above-mentioned cover. Those that choose to home in deeper water and migrate periodically to the feeding grounds may be found resting along some type of migration route (creek channel, timberline, point of land, etc.) very near those prime feeding areas. In this situation concentrate your search around the ten-foot level.

As a footnote on structure, during summer you'll generally find better fishing where the bottom slopes gradually. A sharp drop cannot harbor as many fish at a given depth, because it lacks not only area, but quality of cover as well. Migrating bass don't mind travelling a few hundred yards up a gentle slope to feed during warm water periods, while in the colder months they do.

CONCLUSION

In this example the most productive pattern is clear-cut: Fish the best shallow-water cover during the hours of dusk to dawn. If you aren't sure where those better feeding grounds are, spend a night or two skipping from one prospect to the next and hit each with a variety of techniques and lures. A good place to start is at the back of a weedy or brushy cove. Then work out along the side with the least incline or along the channel if one exists. Be sure to give rocky areas a good going over with crayfish-imitating lures.

Although the fishing may not be as good, during the day you should follow the same pattern on lakes with ample shallow cover. If your waters are barren or the above-mentioned pattern fails, look for those migration routes from feeding grounds to some homing structure in about 10 feet of water. A time-tested trick is to point your bow toward the upper end of the lake where the water is often murkier. Bass do not necessarily migrate to these regions, but the ones residing there will be shallower, due to the reduction of the sun's penetration, and easier to fish for.

LATE SUMMER

Those lucky enough to have the combination of a good bass supply, few fellow anglers and clean water probably will find little difference between early and late summer. The rest of us will. Gradually, the fishing turns poor, sometimes to the point where even the most avid bass angler defects to another sport. To be honest, there is no super system to remedy this condition. But understanding the problem is the first and most important step to reaching a solution.

Lack of Lunkers. Relatively speaking, lunkers are few and far between in any lake at any time. But as the growing season draws to a close, their numbers are really low. That reduces the primary element most anglers need for "good' bassing. March through June is the most lethal period for big bass, with some falling to natural mortality brought on by the rigors of spawning and others to predation by man. By July there may be more lunkers in your memory than in your favorite waters.

Consider these facts. According to numerous studies by fisheries biologists and managers, you are very fortunate if your lake has 50 pounds of bass per acre. Most average only 20. Now, of that 50-pound total, only about 30 pounds (60 percent) will be bass 12 inches or longer. And only five to eight of those 50 pounds belong to bass over three pounds! That means that in a balanced one-acre pond with an excellent bass population you could wipe out the lunkers with one or two casts.

Angling pressure certainly can take its toll. For example, in January, 1966, a census of the bass population in Pony Express Lake, Missouri (240 acres) revealed that 62 percent were 12 inches or longer. Another sampling in October of that same year (the first year fishing was allowed) showed that only *two percent* were in the 12-inch or longer category. Angling pressure was determined the culprit, as it has in many similar studies.

Chances are your water has few lunkers to begin with, and by late summer, after four of the year's most popular fishing months, there may be practically none.

Lure competition. Many things can cause a bass to strike a lure, but the two most important are *hunger*, which is especially stimulating to his appetite when his fat reserve is low, and the presence of *easily accessible food*. In the early spring just about every bass is famished. That's a plus for us fishermen. But since the lake's food supply is at its lowest of the year, the bass find it fruitless to really enter a positive feeding mood. And that's a minus. However, by late spring or early summer when most fish in the lake have spawned and the crayfish are out in full force, the water is suddenly loaded with edibles. Now everything is positive for feeding, and the bass fisherman finds the finest action of the year.

By late summer the bass' fat reserve has been restored and his incentive to feed declines, even though the food supply is still fairly good. This means your artificial lure is now competing with the real thing, and for the affections of an indifferent suitor.

The Disturbance Factor. This problem requires little explanation. In the "good old summertime" households empty and lakes fill with bodies. Fishermen, boaters, skiers, swimmers, sailors, dogs and rock-throwing kids are everywhere. All this commotion drives at least some bass out of their normal routines into unpredictability.

Poor Water Conditions. The warmer the water becomes, the less oxygen it can hold. That single law of nature can play havoc on many waters in late summer, because fish need more oxygen in warm water. In lakes with poor water clarity this "oxygen/temperature tension" may become so severe by July or August that a "summer kill" can result. The fish suffocate.

Fortunately, this is rare, but it calls attention to the fact that conditions may become poor enough to force bass to limit their activity — the degree depending on the severity.

SOME POSSIBLE SOLUTIONS

Go After a Cold Front. This may bristle the back of your neck, as you've undoubtedly been indoctrinated since Day One on the adverse effects of cold fronts on fishing. The truth is that a crispy cool snap in the heat of summer can perk up the bass. The lake's upper layers cool a few degrees to a more favorable temperature and at the same time are able to hold more oxygen. Provided an "oxygen/temperature tension" had been occuring for at least a few days (I've seen them last for weeks) this passing front may bring about some of the year's best fishing. Its tenure, unfortunately, is usually very short.

The best way to learn if your lake is experiencing a "tension" is with an electric thermometer and oxygen monitor. By taking the readings at every foot and recording them, you'll have your answer in about a minute. (See the "Oxygen Requirement Table in Chapter Two.) Without these instruments you can't really know for sure. Still, you can get an idea from just looking into the water. The murkier it is on the year-round average, the greater its chance for a critical "oxygen/temperature tension" during a prolonged summer heat wave. If you can usually see a lure a minimum of four feet down, you're probably safe.

Go at Night. This can counteract most summer problems. The shallows often cool somewhat after sunset, making them more tolerable to a hungry bass. Nighttime also means all that topside commotion is home where it belongs, licking their sunburns. So a bass can roam the shallows without fear. Finally, many of those free-swimming baitfish of daytime are now tucked quietly into dense cover, making themselves as unavailable for dinner as possible. So, with the competition in bed, a phony offering stands a better chance of being assailed.

Abandon the Shallows. Because the shallows are the most productive waters to fish, most bass anglers have no confidence in going "deep." But the fact is that if a "tension" becomes too severe, the bass—particularly lunkers—simply won't be found in the shallows. They'll move to a depth providing the best combination of oxygen, temperature and structure. Since most of their prey will follow suit, a certain degree of feeding should continue and keep the bass vulnerable to your hook.

Again, there's no better or faster way to find this ideal depth than with electronic fishing aids and the pertinent facts, such as those of the "Oxygen Requirement Table." The procedure and a few examples are presented in Chapter 7. If you prefer the cast-and-pray method, start at known shallow-water feeding areas and slowly work deeper via suspected travel routes, such as creek channels, treelines and long sloping points. Once you find a school of bass, you can verify their depth by taking the bass' body temperature. (See Chapter 6.)

The Sit-Tight Method. Once your scouting turns up a new likely-looking deep-water hole, don't give up if a bass isn't caught right away. If bass are there and the lake is not on the verge of a summer kill, sooner or later they will start hitting. I've tested this sit-and-wait theory many times. On the average, two hours between feeding is the longest. It's best if you can locate about four such holes and just keep making the rounds, giving each at least a 15-minute workout with a variety of lures before shuttling off to the next.

Determining Lunker Populations. It can help to know just how many, if any, lunkers are in your immediate water and their general size. Of course, this is much easier to do on smaller bodies of water, particularly if you fish them regularly.

Using a one-acre farm pond as an example, let's say you occasionally catch a limit of bass. That means there are roughly 30 to 40 pounds of bass within and the pond rates a "good." "Excellent" would mean 50 pounds, which would possibly bring you a limit every time, and "fair" about 20 pounds, or just a couple bass each trip.

Now, what about the size of those bass. A wide variety hints that the pond is in balance. Consequently you could expect 10 to 15 percent of all that pond's bass to be three pounds or over. Applying this to our "good" pond, we come up with a lunker population of three to six pounds. And that's assuming none had recently been taken out by fishermen.

Most frequently-fished bass ponds, however, are not in balance, and produce bass of the same general size — usually sub-lunker. If your waters are like this, chances are their big

159

bass potential is "poor" at best. A stunted population occurs when there are not enough large predators to regulate the far more numerous small fish. Actually small lakes and ponds with *many* big bass may soon be heading for the same problem. Too many lunkers keep the smaller bass from growing by either eating them or consuming the food they require for normal growth. Once those large ones die or are removed, there's an explosion of little ones, which, left unchecked, soon outgrow their environment and become stunted.

In a nutshell, a balanced pond holds the best long-term lunker potential. And the best way to keep it like that is not to disrupt any part of it. Throw back the bass you catch, and see that others do the same. If it weren't for catch-and-release programs, such as the "Don't Kill Your Catch" movement organized by Bass Anglers Sportsman Society a few years ago, this country's bass population would be much lower today.

On the other hand, if all your pond gives up are small stunted bass, you should keep some of them and restock with bigger ones. And, if too many lunkers is the problem (problem?) you'd be wise to cull out a few and replace them with smaller bass of various sizes. This will help insure the presence of lunkers for many years to come. With the ever-increasing pressure on bass today, perhaps your best late-summer tactic is *management*.

Chapter 14
Fall and Winter
Water: 75 Degrees to Yearly Lows

It's illogical to go bass fishing in the fall. Catches have been on a downhill skid since mid-summer, and now that the water is cooling, those cold-blooded fish will surely be languid. State Conservation Commission records show that relatively few bass are taken in September and that the ensuing months are progressively worse. A brief stop at your local lake will reveal a sorry number of boat trailers in the parking lots and lonely, untrodden footpaths around the perimeter. Hardly anyone else is fishing, so why should you?

The last guy I know who followed this fashion of reasoning went ice fishing and brought home 50 pounds of ice. You'd be hard-pressed to find a knowledgeable bass fisherman who wouldn't recommend autumn angling. In fact, most feel it's the best time of all. Sure, the water is cooling, but it's that very phenomenon that triggers a strong feeding incentive in the bass. And the state-wide deterioration in the number of bass caught in the fall is explained simply by the drastic drop of rods and reels in motion. It's ironic, because that small percentage of bass fishermen on the water during early-to-mid fall enjoy one of the highest catch rates per hour of the year.

But then, most know what they are doing. Fall fishing has a few idiosyncracies, and it's important to know them. Weather is back as a strong variable, having a lot to do with if and when the bass will hit and their location. Simultaneous patterns can occur from deep water to the shallows, and they may disappear as quickly as they materialized. The food supply is dwindling, the bass are not so finicky and the lunkers return from obscurity.

75 TO 65 DEGREES (EARLY FALL)
September: North — October: South

The transition from late summer to early fall is usually gradual. But occasionally a properly timed Arctic cold front can change weather and water conditions so rapidly that the switch is virtually overnight. If your waters were locked in an "oxygen/temperature tension" prior to this front, you may be in for a couple days of superior fishing. (See Chapter 9.) More than likely, however, it's a series of cold fronts, intermingled with mild warming trends, that slowly brings the upper layers to fall temperatures.

Figure 43 illustrates a common thermal profile of a lake during early fall. Notice that as a whole the water is still showing summer stratification. The only difference is that the shallows have cooled considerably and become more uniform to a greater depth. This makes them ideal for bass, and that almost always translates to mean good fishing.

Locating the Bass. To be perfectly honest, right now is a difficult time to predetermine a pattern. The water is undergoing rapid changes and so is bass behavior. Some will be deep, some will be shallow. Some will be schooled, others scattered. Most will be hungry, a few still not interested. If ever you need to be a flexible, mobile angler, now's the time.

Being so congenial once again, the shallows are where you should concentrate, much as you did in the spring. A favorite

162

EARLY FALL

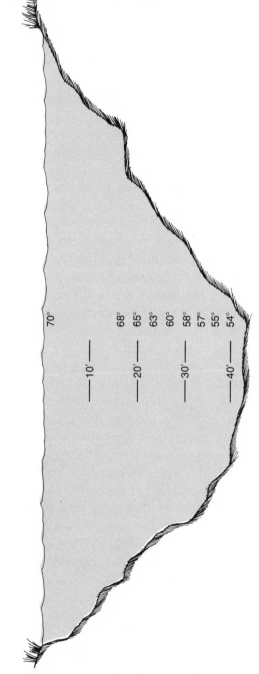

Figure 43. In early fall, the water still shows summer stratification. But the shallows have cooled considerably and become more uniform to a greater depth. This is ideal for bass and makes for good fishing.

163

area is in the back end of coves and river arms with distinct channels. Even if the banks are under only a foot of water, the presence of adequate cover often signals bass. Keep your eyes open for shad or similar baitfish activity around brushy flats near these channels. If cover is sparse, hit the outside bend of the channel and feeder stream intersections. The best deep-water pattern, such as after a front, is along some well-defined structure (breakline, stumpfield, creek channel) on a point. Cold fronts also cause bass to tuck snugly into cover or school tightly in deep water.

Lures and Techniques. Bass aren't very selective now. The food supply is too low. So forget the spoonfeeding tactics of summer and choose a lure that covers a lot of water quickly. Your primary concern is finding the bass, and you can't afford to waste time inching something along the bottom in an uncertain area. A deep-running crankbait or small-bladed spinnerbait is a good scouting lure in the fall. They not only work fast, but imitate the bass' main food source — baitfish.

Give suspected structures about a half-dozen casts, then move on. Keep in mind that on some days at this time of year you may fish for hours without a strike, only to have the water erupt with bass for 30 glorious minutes. If you are on a school and the action suddenly stops, immediately change to a different type of lure. This often brings in a couple more. Try not to get stuck on just one pattern. Establish as many as you can, then pound the one relinquishing the largest fish.

On heavily fished lakes it's common to have difficulty catching bass with conventional methods. During the past six months they have been treated to an endless parade of popular lure types, colors and retrieves, so you may have to dig deeply into your tackle box and imagination. Try that green and pink "Bass-Zapper" that's been stuck to the side of your worm tray for three years. Tie 14 jigs together with piano wire and bounce them sporadically along the bottom. Do anything with anything that the bass have not been conditioned to resist. The results may surprise you.

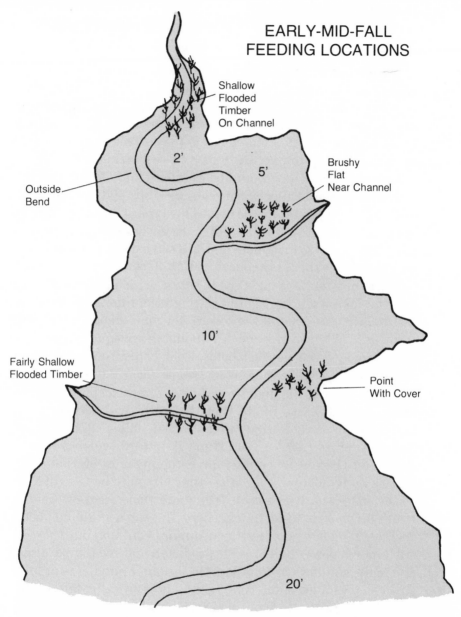

EARLY-MID-FALL
FEEDING LOCATIONS

Shallow
Flooded
Timber
On Channel

Brushy
Flat
Near Channel

Outside
Bend

2'

5'

Fairly Shallow
Flooded Timber

10'

Point
With Cover

20'

Figure 44. A warm, sunny fall day rings the dinner bell for bass as the shallows warm, enticing the baitfish, and the bass.

WATER 64 TO 55 DEGREES (MID-FALL)
October: North — November: South

By now, an average lake in an average year will look something like Figure 45. The bottom-most region may still hold its summer stratification, but for the most part the lake is uniform and well into "fall turnover." On windy or cloudy days you may find little temperature change from the surface down to 30 feet or more, erasing temperature as a bass-locating aid.

A warm, sunny day would be another story. As shown, the extreme shallows may warm considerably and, as a result, draw food and predators to them. This type of day often brings the best fall fishing, just as it did in the early spring. Big bass in particular seem to love them and will settle into choice shallow cover anyplace there is a concentration of food. (See Figure 44.)

Since the bass have had time to adjust to cooler temperatures and the lake itself isn't going through the intense changes of last month, you should see fewer, yet more dependable, patterns now. What works one day should prove equally good the next, provided the weather holds. Cold fronts from now on can be catastrophic since there is no longer a warm upper layer to shield the rest of the lake from changes in atmospheric conditions. It is also less likely that the water will recover completely from a cold front, except when followed by Indian Summer, since the seasonal trend is toward cooler weather. Watch for those warm sunny days, then pounce on them like there's no tomorrow — because that just may be the case.

The more the water cools, the more those heat-of-the-day hours become the best time to fish. The sun's angle has been decreasing steadily since the autumnal equinox, but there is still enough power in its rays to produce a marked temperature rise in the shallows by mid-day. On the other hand, if your lake still receives a lot of daytime fishing pressure this late in the year, or is unusually clear, you may be wise to don your thermal underwear and try at night. This requires pure dedication and the constitution of a plow horse, but many fall trophies are taken under the stars.

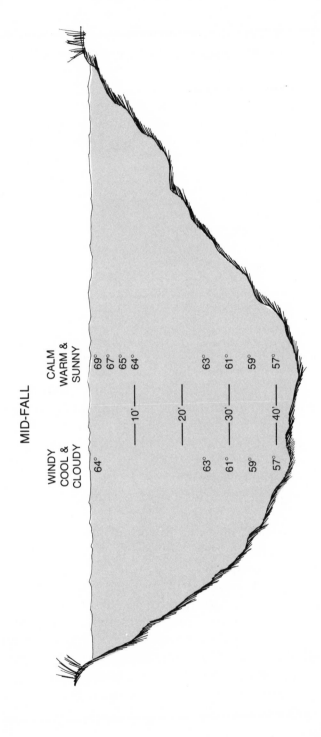

MID-FALL

WINDY
COOL &
CLOUDY

CALM
WARM &
SUNNY

69°
67°
65°
64°

64° ——— 10' ——— 64°

——— 20' ———

63° ——— 30' ——— 63°

61° ——————— 61°

59° ——— 40' ——— 59°

57° ——————— 57°

Figure 45. By mid-fall, the bottom of a lake may still be stratified, but for the most part the lake is uniform and well into "fall turnover."

167

Lures and Techniques. Once water temperatures drop below 60 degrees, it's time to start slowing down the speed of retrieve. Favorites now are spinnerbaits with medium-to-large blades, small crankbaits reeled in slowly and eratically and, of course, plastic worms. Some experts report doing well with "gurgle" baits and standard surface lures. Actually, just about anything has potential, provided it appears as an easy meal to the bass.

You may want to start off with a color, size and action that mimics shad or other baitfish in your lake, since these are about the only entrees of interest left to the bass now. But don't make the mistake of getting hung up on just one lure, color, etc. Experimentation is still the only sure way to find out what your quarry wants.

WATER: 54 TO 45 DEGREES (LATE FALL)
November: North — December: South

The honeymoon is drawing to a close. As water temperatures continue dropping in these latter months, the bass fishing gets tougher. With slowed metabolism, and diminished food supplies, the fish will enter a positive feeding mood no more than once a day, possibly as infrequently as every four days. Lures must often be worked painstakingly slow to induce a strike — and fingers may not work at all. The good news is that the bass' location, the best days to fish, and the most likely biting time of any given day are all more predictable.

On a cloudy day with even a mild breeze the *entire* lake should "turn over," meaning bottom layers will mix with top layers and create thermal uniformity. Consequently, water temperature will be no help in locating the bass. You will have to rely on your knowledge of the lake's structure and past experiences. A calm sunny day, on the other hand, should generate a warm upper layer and bring a few bass up for dinner. More than ever these are the days to go — and mid-day is the time.

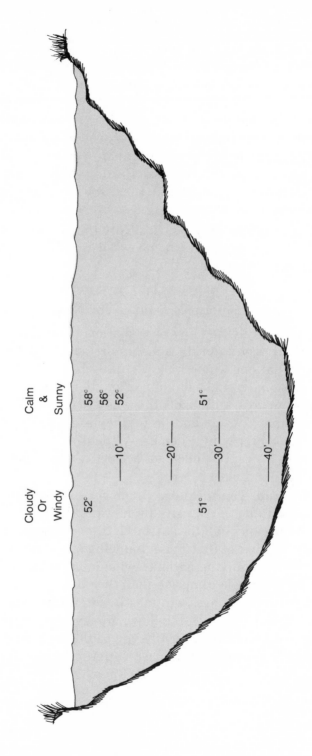

Figure 46. *As water temperatures drop, so does the bass' interest in feeding. They're beginning to school up and settle into their deep-water winter homes.*

As a rule, the bass will be forming into larger schools, beginning to settle around their deep-water winter homes. These will usually be on steeper inclines, which stretch from the shallows to no less than 15 feet in shallow murky lakes and 30 feet in deep clear ones. Good examples are rock bluffs where a creek channel swings in closely, the deep-water side of a point, a dam's rip-rap or in the lower branches of certain submerged trees. (See Figure 47.) Whether the day calls for working the shallows or the depths, confine your search to these immediate areas.

Lures and Techinques. Basically there is little difference in this category between late fall and winter. So, see the following section: "Winter."

WATER: ANNUAL LOWS (WINTER)
50 Degrees: South — Ice: North

You will rarely find any bass shallow now. Those warming trends that used to bring some up are so few and meager by January that one would have virtually no effect. At best, you may occasionally find a handful of smaller bass temporarily in the medium layers, probably there as a result of hunger rather than weather. But by and large, they are schooled tightly in their deep-water winter homes. Without a doubt, this time of year makes a depth-finder, an accurate map and familiarity with the lake almost a must.

Lures and Techniques. From spring through fall, the most important prerequisite by far was finding the bass. In winter that's only half the battle. Getting a lure down to where it's right in front of their nose, inducing one to hit it, knowing when one does, having patience when none does, and keeping warm all the while comprise the other half.

The depth of the bass will mostly determine what lure you choose. If your lake is the shallow, murky type where the bass winter at 15 feet, theoretically you could use a plastic worm, spinnerbait or even certain deep-running crankbaits. In most waters, however, the bass will be anywhere from 25 to 60 feet

170

LATE FALL AND WINTER
DEEP-WATER HOMES

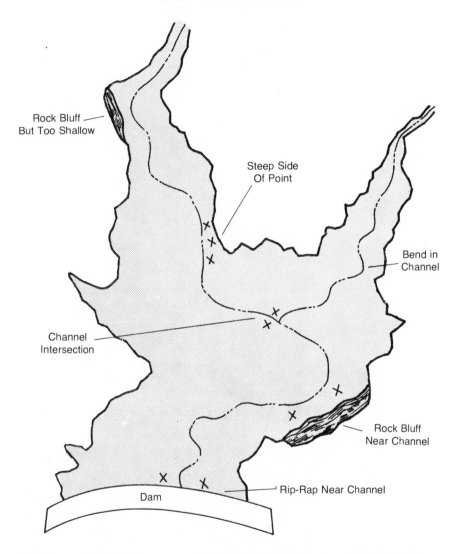

Figure 47. Good Places to Look for Bass. Winter homes will usually be on steeper inclines, around rock bluffs near a channel and on the deep-water side of a point.

171

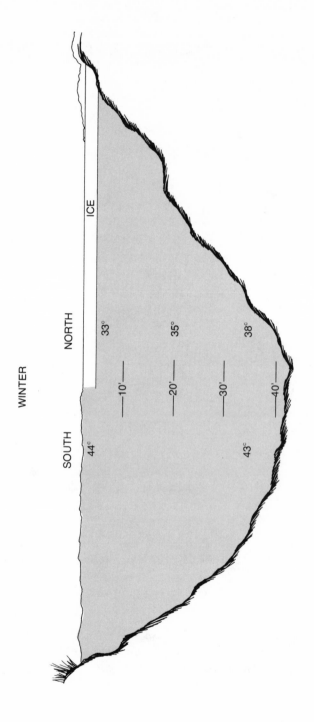

WINTER

SOUTH   NORTH

ICE

44°

10'

20'

30'

40'

33°

35°

38°

43°

Figure 48. The bass are deep, schooled tightly and tough to find without a depth-finder, an accurate map and familiarity with the lake.

deep, and that's a different ball game. Vertical jigging is probably the best method and calls for something that sinks quickly and is heavy enough to keep your line tight in this much water for proper "feel." Bass strike so lightly during winter that keen concentration and constant contact with the lure are imperative. The better lures are the metal jigging types, such as half-ounce jigs and jigging spoons, the jig-n-eel, tail-spinners and single-spins.

Via anchor, trolling motor or — for the northern soul — ice augur, hold right over the school and lower your selection to the bottom. With the rod tip no more than six inches above the water, reel in any slack. Next, with a slow, sweeping motion, raise the rod tip three or four feet, then lower it back to the original position, taking special care to keep tension on the line at all times. Otherwise, a strike may go undetected. Repeat several thousand times. The other method on open water is to hold the boat slightly back from the school, cast as far as you can across it, let the lure sink, then jig it along the bottom until you reach the bass.

WINTER'S END

You haven't seen water in months. Memories have been your only sustenance, but lately they've become fuzzy and stale. Both you and your August trophy have put on weight since then, and cabin fever has you washing the landing net. Your fishing buddy called the other day with nothing to say.

Then something strange comes slowly rolling up from the south. There's an odor on the winds once again; it's someone's barnyard thawing out, but it smells sweet just the same. The earth is humming. A billion feisty bass begin swimming up your veins. Winter wasn't so long after all.

Out comes your gear. Fifteen spiders run for their lives. How good it is to see all those cherished, bass-nabbing lures again, 80 percent of which have never been wet. Your favorite rods and reels — abused all year, then thrown behind the den door — are now cleaned with so much tender loving care, that muffled laughter is coming from the kitchen.

Undaunted, you retrieve your fishing cap from the kids' toy box, your patch jacket from the closet, and boots from the back porch. The door doesn't quite close. The car starts. Tires squeal. Your wife shakes her head.

Another revolution completed.

The cycle goes on.

Index